Are You Ready to Teach Belly Dance?

Paving the Way to Success

TAAJ

ISBN: 0974120847
ISBN-13: 978-0-9741208-4-3

DEDICATION

For those who dare to live their dreams.

CONTENTS

INTRODUCTION

The road to teaching belly dance has gone from being a meager little trail to a buzzing boulevard. It starts out with becoming a student. Then you hit a crossroad where one way leads to The Land of Teaching and the other continues on the student path. Here you have to decide whether to continue on as a student or to turn off. You encounter this same option over and over. Whenever anyone finds out that you dance, you hear, "Can you teach me to do that?" When you perform the call is even louder.

Sometimes you hit that crossroad early when you're not experienced enough to know what lays down that dark and scary turn. You're full of enthusiasm and ignorance and bounce joyfully into the unknown because after all, what could it hurt? It's *just* a belly dance class. Even if you don't particularly *want* to teach, you may consider that route because it's the next logical thing. It's what expected.

Or maybe you are the student who passes up the opportunity because you lack the confidence. The idea of teaching others seems too big and important for you to imagine that you could do it successfully. You might get there someday, but you see it as being far, far into the future.

Or maybe you have a dance background in another genre. You've taught that successfully. You are wondering how hard can it be to add belly dance to your class offerings?

Are You Ready to Teach Belly Dance? is for the student who is faced with the decision and wondering, "Is this for me? Is now a good time? Is this in my future?" As with anything in life, when you make a fully-informed, conscious choice, you are more likely to find peace and success.

DO YOU REALLY *WANT* TO TEACH?

Before you jump into teaching, it's a good first step to mindfully decide if it's something you even want to do. Don't just do it because your teacher needs the help or it seems like the natural next step. If you are going to do it well and enjoy it, it has to be something you *want* to do.

So, what does it mean to *mindfully* decide? In mindfulness, there are three states of mind: the emotion mind, the reasonable mind, and the wise mind. The emotion mind is the part of us that feels. It sends us messages through the body. When we are happy, our body feels light and buoyant. Our faces smile. Our hearts sing. When we are angry, our chest constricts. Our breathing quickens. Our head may feel tight or hot. There are other physical states associated with different emotional states.

Emotion mind is useful because love, excitement, and happiness make life worth living. They give us a sense of reward and pleasure. Feelings like anxiety, anger, and fear let us know that something is wrong and we need to make adjustments.

Reasonable mind is the part of us that calculates or thinks. Reasonable mind uses the logic to help us resolve issues like

1

balancing a checkbook, getting from point A to B, or creating a schedule. You certainly *could* use emotional mind for these tasks, but reasonable mind is generally more effective because it considers things like time, finances, and efficiency over things like whimsy, impulse, and fear, which is the dominion of emotional mind. The choices of the reasonable mind tend to be practical.

Wise mind is that calm, still place inside of us that is so finely tuned into us and the environment that it never steers us wrong. Women's intuition and hunches come from this place. You can think of the emotional mind as the heart, the reasonable mind as the brain, and the wise mind as the gut.

As you think of the question of whether or not you want to teach, what does your gut say? If your gut says no, you're done. LISTEN! Remember that this is the voice of the calm, still place inside of you that *never steers you wrong*. If you are still not sure, read on.

A LOOK AT THE JOB

Work Hours

Most classes take place during evenings and weekends. Most people work during the day, so evenings and weekends are when they are available for other things. Evenings are also when social gatherings, PTA meetings, sports games, parenting time, dating, dinner, studying, and shopping usually take place. Do you have enough time to add one more activity? Will you have to abandon activities on a regular basis that you don't want to give up?

If you have small children, a demanding full-time career, a hobby that requires a lot of time, or many family obligations, you will need to consider this. Teaching is a commitment that will most likely take away from your ability to do other things you enjoy. These responsibilities don't necessarily mean you *can't* teach. Maybe it means limiting your instruction to one class with no extras. Having a balanced work, family, and personal life makes all areas of your life happier and more fulfilling. When you plan for all aspects of your life, you are more likely to maintain a happy, balanced life.

Pay

If you are teaching at a recreation center, fitness center, or similar facility, it's fairly common to be paid an hourly wage. Sounds like a good deal, right? Let's say you are paid $20 per hour to teach a one-hour class. Add to that the time it takes you to get to the class and home. If you arrive early or stay late to talk to students, add that time too. Add class prep time. How much are you being paid for your time now?

The hourly pay option might work out if you teach several classes back to back, but if it's just one class, you will be lucky to make minimum wage! Quite often it's not enough to cover gas and childcare. If teaching is the only income you expect from this job (in other words, you are not selling products) and money is an important issue, you would be better off taking a part-time job elsewhere.

Of course, pay can be negotiable. If you are being hired to teach, you could ask for a split of the total fees. If your classes are well attended, you will make out much better with this arrangement. Let me show you.

Let's say that you have the option of getting $20 per hour or a 50/50 split for a single class that runs for eight weeks. There are ten students who pay $100 each. If you took the hourly rate, you would earn $160 before taxes. After the studio paid you, it kept $840. If you took the 50/50 split, you would both make $500. Which is the better deal for you?

I used the example of having ten students because that is an achievable goal for any class. If you have a class that's jammed to the gills, your potential income increases tremendously!

Another option is to rent studio space. Around here, the going rate is $40 per hour. Some classes are back to back and you don't have the luxury of having cushion time. If I am renting space, I like to have the studio fifteen minutes before the start of the class and fifteen minutes after. It feels less rushed and I can talk to my students that way.

Let's use the same example of ten students in an eight-week session who pay $100 each. My studio rent for that time period is $400. I gross $1,000, so what's left over after expenses is $600.

So, depending on the scenario, I can make $160, $500, or $600 for the same job! Why not get the most money for the same amount of time?

When I started dancing in Virginia in 1996, classes were $10 a week. I see classes now advertised for $5 a week. If you don't value what you do, your students won't either. If you are going to teach, *please, please, please* ask for a decent wage. When you offer prices that aren't in keeping with industry standards, you lower the standard of living for teachers who depend on this work for their living. If your community can't afford the going rate, perhaps it can't afford you.

I don't know anyone whose Get Rich Quick scheme includes teaching belly dance. Still, a girl's got to eat! You have to consider this when deciding whether it makes sense for you to start teaching.

Time Investment

I already talked about the time it takes to get to the job, but you will also spend time outside the classroom planning and preparing for classes. A new teacher will spend much more time on this than a seasoned one, so factor that in. A teacher with students who perform a lot or one who has a troupe, will invest even more.

Here are some of the unpaid class prep tasks I spend time on:

- finding video clips
- copying hand-out and sign-in sheets
- sewing parties
- video parties
- scouting out performing opportunities
- creating choreographies
- creating lesson plans
- tracking down costuming
- looking for recital space
- editing music for class and performances
- listening to and buying new music for class

You may have more or fewer unpaid activities, but these types of things should be considered if you make the decision to teach. You may be committing to much more than the hours you spend in the classroom. In fact, most teachers will invest at least one hour for every "in class" hour. Do you have that kind of time?

It's important to consider money and time. Teaching is a job that pays you only for the time you spend with your students. The only way to increase your pay is to increase the number of students, increase the number of hours you spend with students, or create passive income. The first two options almost always mean that you will also increase the number of unpaid hours you spend working. You have to figure out if the money and other benefits are worth the pay and investment of time.

Your Dance Progress

When I started teaching, my personal practice time suffered. I didn't have time to work on my own skills because I spent all my dance time working on dances for my students or on developing the studio. I find this is true for many teachers. The more involved you are with your classes, the less time you may have for your own development.

If your own dance progress is important to you, be sure to factor in the amount of time that you need to keep developing *your* dance. Consider not just time, but energy. Will you have the stamina to rehearse after all the hours you put in on student development? If you don't want to take a chance on your own performance suffering, think about this before you begin teaching. Instructors in other dance forms understand this very well. I believe this is why so many of them wait until their performing days are over to begin teaching.

My advice is, if you still have professional *performing* goals, don't teach. The time you invest in developing your students will inhibit your ability to reach those goals.

Friendships

Many of us are drawn to the dance community for the wonderful feeling of camaraderie we get with the other women we find here. Beware! That is hard to sustain if you are "the boss." It's hard to be friends with your students if you want to run a business. I am not saying that you can't be *friendly*. It helps your business to be friendly and likable. It can hurt your business to be peers.

As a business owner, you are the CEO. You are going to have to make decisions about who gets to move up to the next level, who gets to dance in the front row, who gets to solo, and things like that. These may seem like unimportant decisions; however, if you make decisions your friends don't like, you may be asked to choose between your friendship and your business.

Your friend is going to want you to support her no matter what. Your business demands that you do what's right and fair for the class. If your rule is that a dancer can't perform once she has missed a certain number of classes, and your friend "Jamila" has hit that number, you will have to act. It doesn't matter if you know that Jamila is having family problems. The class doesn't want favoritism. They want to know that they have the same responsibilities and consequences as the next student.

Jamila, however, wants to know that she can count on your support when she's down. Your role as friend and teacher are in conflict. You may not be able to do what's right for your friend and your business. Someone is probably going to be hurt.

If friendships are important to you, and you still want to teach, don't teach your friends. Don't cultivate friendships with your students. Most successful instructors have strong boundaries between friends, students, co-workers, and clients. Belly dance is a business. When we treat it as a hobby, the integrity of the art suffers because we risk lowering our standards to accommodate our friends.

Competition

Despite the lip service given to this wonderful sisterhood of belly dance, there are people who see other dancers and instructors as competition. There are two things to think about where that is concerned. First, is there truly enough demand for another teacher (or can this be created)? Second, do you want to be on the receiving end of petty jealousies?

I see no problem with more businesses entering the field because I don't think that someone in the same business needs to be seen as competition. After all, you aren't offering exactly the same thing, are you? Studies have proven that if you are in a community where two people provide the same product or service, both do better than if there were only one. This means that your competition isn't competition at all, but an asset. If you work together to create excitement about the dance, the benefit increases even more. If you approach the dance with the attitude that there is enough business and opportunity for everybody, there will be. We always get back the energy we send out.

On the other hand, you may have different values. Maybe you see starting a new class as being disloyal to existing teachers. Maybe the thought of someone not approving of your choice to teach is distasteful to you. If this is a situation that makes you uncomfortable, think about it. It's hard to give energy to things that you don't believe in.

As for rivalries and jealousies, this can be very damaging. If you are pretty, young, fit, enthusiastic, good at what you do, or have any qualities that make you stand out from the crowd, you are going to be a target. This is not about being pessimistic. It's about facing the truth. Performing arts can be a cutthroat business. Some people don't like sharing the limelight and (wrongly) believe that if you weren't there, they'd have more. I've seen many women leave the dance because of this. Again, it's not something that means you *can't* follow your dream. It may be something that you want to think about as you decide if and how you want to embark on a teaching career.

Intrinsic Rewards

I took a break from teaching for a while. When I came back I decided that my focus would be helping other aspiring dancers achieve their goals. Each month my intermediate class worked on a different subject area or concept. As you might imagine, the first week was hard. They struggled, but as time passed, they grew comfortable with the material and started to make it their own.

There is something special about watching that happen. I am so fulfilled to know that I had something to do with it. I'm not taking the credit. I just gave the seed and the student turned it into something. That's very rewarding to see.

That is just one of the many intrinsic rewards that come from teaching. Teaching is an incredible gift. It's also a big responsibility. You're giving something that cannot be taken away. You may find that this is something that factors into your desire to teach (or not to teach). If there is no intrinsic reward, it's probably not a good time to teach. The demands are high and the other rewards for most of us are few and far between.

External Rewards

I don't see anything wrong with teaching for external reward. After all, we don't enjoy or continue to do things for which there is no gain. Payment is one external reward. Others could be recognition of your talent, advancement of your career, or documentation of your work through the performances of others.

Working *solely* for external reward doesn't tend to bring out our best work, but it should be a part of the decision making process. It's reasonable to expect that you will get something in return for your investment. If you aren't getting anything out of it, why bother?

OTHER TASKS

Obviously the main work of a teacher is to teach, but teaching requires that you handle other tasks as well. Let's take a look at them and see what else goes along with the job.

Paper pusher Being a paper pusher means that you are responsible for setting up your business structure (business license, tax identification number, establishing a business entity), creating a business plan, creating a budget, paying invoices, filing taxes, keeping track of business expenses, writing contracts, creating policies, collecting fees, and other administrative tasks. Your role as paper pusher will vary greatly depending upon your situation. An employee will have a lot less responsibility -- perhaps even none.

Marketer Even if you work for someone else, you will want to get the word out about your classes, keep current students happy, and attract new ones. This means you have to know who your market is, make efforts to reach it, and create regular contact with your clients and potential client base.

Babysitter/Counselor Performing arts is an emotional business. Many people put their hearts and souls into their work. When it doesn't go as well as they'd like, the situation can get emotional. Sometimes it's reasonable disappointment.

Sometimes the issues are irrational and ego-based. This means that you will sometimes get called in to resolve personal and interpersonal disputes. If you like high drama or prefer to avoid conflict altogether, this may be something to spend some time thinking about. You may not think of dance teachers as therapists, but at times this is exactly what is called for. Are you up for the challenge?

Planner So much of what goes on in a well-run classroom is prepared in advance: lesson plans, choreographies, schedules, recital rehearsals, show line-ups, costume creation, and more. The more organized you are, the better your class will function.

Seamstress It's not your job to teach people how to sew or to do any sewing for them, but let's face it. If you don't help your new students, where are they going to learn? Even if you buy all your costuming there are always alterations to be made.

Disciplinarian Your students take their cue from you. If you fly by the seat of your pants, they will too. This doesn't usually make for smooth sailing in any way. Your job is to set and enforce the rules and policies. You can get by without doing this. Plenty of teachers do. However, their classrooms are not particularly productive. In the end, that makes more work for you and less satisfaction for the student.

Choreographer Teaching, performing, and creating choreography are three very different skill sets. It's rare to find a person who does all three well, yet in belly dance, all three are demanded of instructors. Students want to walk away from classes with something tangible to show their family and friends. It's your job to give that to them.

Choreography can be avoided, but it's something most students demand. You will drastically restrict your income if you cut it out completely.

Webmaster Having a website isn't a requirement for any business; however, your ability to do business will be very much handicapped if you don't have a good one. If you have someone create it for you and aren't able to update it yourself, it will be a very expensive proposition. It's best to have at least rudimentary webmaster skills.

Audio Technician Classes move a lot more smoothly if you have your audios cued and cut the way you will need them in class. For instance, if I am teaching a choreography and want to review a particular block of music four times before adding the next block, it is a lot easier to isolate that block than to start at the beginning and fast forward each time. If the next section includes the first and second sections, I generally create a file with just that music on it. That requires time, effort and know-how, yet saves time and effort in the classroom.

Bill Collector Having solid payment policies keeps this from being an issue, but I have known some teachers who get into problems with past-due payments and bounced checks.

Networker This is another optional task. Taking on the role of networker can make you more visible, more popular, and more successful. It is a lot easier to work with others to than to go it alone.

Since you likely will spend at least one hour per week on nonteaching tasks, it pays to be good at and like some of them. If you have a way to delegate the ones you don't like, and can afford to do so, that may be a better use of your time.

Do You Really Want to Teach?

There may additional issues that influence your decision to teach (like political climate, availability of other teachers, continuing training opportunities, etc). I just wanted to introduce some of the major things that may play a role in your decision-making. When we think about what we are doing and have information about it beforehand, we are usually more prepared to see our decision through without regret.

Considering all the preceding points, do you really *want* to teach? Sometimes the idea of teaching is more attractive than the reality. Or maybe you like it a lot, and now is not the best time. Perhaps reading this helps you to see that teaching is something you must do. Or maybe you are still undecided. If so, keep reading. There is much more to consider.

ARE YOU QUALIFIED TO TEACH?

If you went through everything in "Do You Really *Want* to Teach" and are still reading, I assume the following is true:

- The work hours and pay are acceptable
- You have the time to devote to teaching
- You have worked out a way to minimize impact to your own dance development
- You have a plan for preserving friendships and your business
- You envision getting some type of reward that makes the investment of time worthwhile
- You feel you can handle the "competition."
- Your business skills are up to par

While that's a great start, that's not all you need. Now let's take a closer look at you to see if you have the necessary skills to do a good job.

Personal Skills

Discipline

Teaching is a profession. It's a business. You have to remain ahead of the student. You have to keep new students coming in and keep the old ones happy. That doesn't happen by accident. It takes a solid plan and the discipline to stick with it.

When I say that a teacher should be "disciplined," I mean that she needs a method of working that continues until good cause is shown to modify the plan. If Friday afternoon is administrative work time, that should happen every Friday afternoon. If the budget for advertising is X, it should stay at X. If the policy is that a student must be at least 13 to take classes, the policy should stand.

A disciplined business plan is prioritized. New projects are not taken on until old ones are completed. Energy is focused, not scattered. No new commitments are taken on until all aspects are considered and it is assured that there are enough time and resources to complete them, and the rewards are worth the expenditure. Having a disciplined work strategy keeps everything progressing in an orderly way.

The teaching strategy is also disciplined. It is systematic and well thought out. There is a discernible beginning and end to lessons. There are delineations between students of varying skill levels. There is order in the classroom. There has to be a planned goal, a way to get there, and someone strong to keep things on track. Without this, your class will be just a hobby or a club because the students will find it hard to advance their skills.

I realize that belly dance is an artistic endeavor and the type of things I am talking about are left brain tasks. That might make it challenging for artistic types, but in order to have a class that grows and thrives, you must be organized and disciplined. It doesn't happen by chance. It happens through planning.

I am not saying that a creative, spontaneous person can't teach. I am saying that that type of personality will have a hard time teaching successfully if creativity alone is used. There is just too much room for forgetting, neglecting, and not completing things if there is no discipline. Eventually this leads to big mistakes.

Good Interpersonal Skills

Many personality types can succeed as belly dance teachers. I don't think that an introvert has an advantage over an extrovert or an intellectual is superior to someone who is more emotional. However, there are some interpersonal skills that make it easier to succeed as a teacher. The first is flexibility.

For example, teachers have to deal with students with differing communication needs. Some will need detailed, concrete feedback while others will shrink if you make a vague correction that they interpret as saying they did something wrong. It's up to you to tune in to the needs of your class and alter your communication style to fit the person you are talking to. You are the leader. A "one size fits all" approach will not work if you want to keep all your students challenged and happy. You cannot expect the class to adapt to you.

Flexibility with communication style is important, but you also need flexibility in other areas. Some students crave the limelight while others are content to hide in the crowd.

Can these people work well in the same classroom? How will you handle that in a way that's fair, yet makes everyone comfortable? When you know in advance that people are different, have different needs, and you are willing to work with that, you will be less frazzled at the end of the day.

Another beneficial interpersonal skill is the ability to nurture and develop talent. A student can be taught by ridicule and abuse. Many old ballet masters have reputations for being cruel, yet they produced talented artists. However, this is not my idea of a *good* teacher. A good teacher inspires excellence by *balancing* praise with constructive criticism. Going overboard with praise may make a student feel good, but it also gives a false impression of greatness. This does the student no real favors. It sets her up for disappointment when she realizes eventually that her skills are not all that fantastic.

Condemnation discourages. It could make someone who has a slow start drop out before she's had a chance to blossom. A good teacher is able to accurately express what a student is doing wrong, help her to make the changes she needs to make, and positively acknowledges her progress. Her comments are helpful and honest, yet encouraging.

A good teacher is able to diffuse outbursts and conflicts. She keeps class focused on instruction and immediately takes care of any disruptions. She gently shows that she is the boss and can be assertive if she needs to, but always treats everyone with respect. By giving the student the type of feedback she needs, respecting her personal preferences about performing while being fair to the entire class, honestly assessing ability and encouraging growth, and keeping control of the classroom, the teacher builds trust. Students stay with a teacher they trust.

Balanced Ego

If you have been involved in belly dance for any length of time, you know that there are instructors, troupe directors, choreographers, and students who are destructive to be around. Maybe they have low self-esteem, experience anxiety, or a have a streak of perfectionism. Maybe they were abused as children or perhaps are in an abusive situation currently. Maybe they experience emotional or physical pain. Whatever the circumstances, they lack the ability to deal with it constructively and it comes out in harmful ways.

Sometimes the students are held back by loyalty to a teacher who doesn't give them the confidence to see themselves as soloists or professionals. Sometimes the students are held back by lack of opportunity to shine. The instructor uses them as background dancers or in shows that don't stretch their skills. Perhaps the instructor is outright mean. I've seen that too! A single caustic comment can cause a student to drop out or lose all confidence,.

Like many professionals, belly dance instructors have a lot of power to enhance or damage people's lives. Many students idolize their teachers and put them on a pedestal. That power and admiration can be seductive. If you are in a place where you need some help, please get it. While we are not physicians who take an oath to do no harm, we are fellow human beings who, I hope, have that as part of our personal ethics.

There is nothing wrong with being appreciated or loving to be loved. There is something wrong with hurting other people in order to get that. If the attraction of being admired puts you in a bad place, please get some help before placing fragile egos in your hands.

Education

Cultural/Historical Knowledge

The longer I stay in belly dance, I realize that the more I know, the less I know. Beliefs that I developed by listening to reputable sources are challenged. There are differing opinions about this and that. New information comes to light. Even the natives don't necessarily know their own history, so how is a belly dance teacher supposed to know whether she knows enough cultural and historical information to be a good teacher? Where does one draw the line?

That's a tough thing to answer. There certainly is more to know than one can ever learn in a lifetime, particularly if you are independently verifying each fact before presenting it to others. So, my standard of "how much cultural/historical knowledge do you have to know before you are qualified to teach" is "enough that you can confidently answer commonly asked questions and perform pieces in your repertoire in a culturally accurate way." You must also have enough knowledge to be able either to quickly locate a reliable human resource or reputable documented resource for the answer.

Belly dance is a folk dance. As a teacher of a folk dance, you are responsible for accurately preserving and portraying that culture. You should be able to identify regional variations by eye and ear. You should be able to distinguish folklore from fakelore and correctly label what you are seeing. If you can't identify what you are seeing, you won't be able to find a resource for answers about it or refer the student to a more knowledgeable resource. You may pass along fantasy as something authentic and spread ignorance.

So what is the standard of proof when trying to verify a cultural or historical fact? Well, some things are easier to verify than others. The stories that the dance has a history in the temples and that Gypsies danced with swords to charm soldiers so that they could be robbed are frequently told, but that doesn't make it so.

When I am faced with a question regarding an oft-told tale, I may repeat it, but I'll preface it with, "Legend says ..." I may also end it with, "... but verify that for yourself." I will also attempt to find trustworthy evidence either to support or to refute it. Some tales are interesting to tell, but why spread mythology if you can counter it with truth? If you know that there are contradicting stories circulating about a topic, cite the source for your beliefs. You can respond to the question with something like, "The jury is still out on that, but Scholar A says, 'blah, blah, blah' and This Authority says, 'blah, blah, blah' so the evidence indicates that this is probably true/not true." You don't have to be an authority. You just have to have a reasonable level of knowledge and a source to back it up.

There are many ways to gain cultural and historical knowledge. One is to talk to human resources, also known as people! I haven't met a Middle Eastern person yet who doesn't want to share stories about his or her homeland. You may find that many sources contradict each other, but life is like that. That is the nature of culture. It's not homogeneous.

If you like reading, here are some books that I recommend for boosting your historical and cultural knowledge:

Buonaventura, Wendy. *Serpent of the Nile: Women and Dance in the Arab World*. Interlink Publishing Group, 2009.

Carlton, Donna. *Looking for Little Egypt*. International Dance Discovery, 1995.

Fonseca, Isabel. *Bury Me Standing: The Gypsies and Their Journey*. Vintage, 1996.

Lexova, Irena, Diane Bergman, K. Haltmar, *Ancient Egyptian Dances*. Dover Publications, 1999.

Morocco. *You Asked Aunt Rocky: Answers and Advice about Raqs Sharqi and Raqs Shaabi*. RDI Publications, 2013.

Redmond, Layne. *When the Drummers Were Women: A Spiritual History of Rhythm*. Three Rivers Press, 1997.

Richards, Tazz, Kajira Djoumahna. *The Belly Dance Book: Rediscovering the Oldest Dance*. Backbeat Press, 2000.

Shay, Anthony., Barbara Sellers-Young. Belly Dance: *Orientalism, Transnationalism, and Harem Fantasy*. Mazda Publications, 2005.

Stewart, Iris, J. *Sacred Woman, Sacred Dance: Awakening Spirituality Through Movement & Ritual*. Inner Traditions, 2013.

Van Nieuwkerk, Karin. *A Trade Like Any Other: Female Singers and Dancers in Egypt*. University of Texas Press, 1996.

Another way to increase your cultural and historical knowledge is to take classes in folkloric styles of dance from the established leaders *of that particular style*. Don't go just for name recognition. A well-known teacher may be good at some things, but not necessarily good at teaching what you want. A not-so-well-known teacher *could* be the diamond in the rough that puts it all together for you. Don't take it for granted that Name = Knowledge, No Name = Nothing. Ask people you respect. They will give you the straight scoop.

You can also pose questions on internet bulletin boards. There are forums for just about everything you could ever want to know. Sites have members ranging from beginner to professional. The population spans the globe. The topics cover everything from performing to shopping. Some contributors are very knowledgeable and helpful, so take advantage of this. Most people are very willing to share.

If you have Middle Eastern owned restaurants or clubs with Middle Eastern food in your area, check them out. Experience the food. Listen to the music. Watch the natives dance. Take in the atmosphere. This is how I learned the bulk of what I know. Experiencing everything in context fills in the picture in a way that no book or class can.

If you have the time and the means, take a tour to Egypt, Turkey or some other country where dance is in abundance. If you can go on a dancer tour, so much the better! A dancer tour can get you in places that a commercial tour would not even dream of taking you. The workshops, shows, and shopping are unparalleled. The experience will be well worth the investment. My entire understanding of dance changed as a result of going to Egypt.

The bottom line about cultural and historical knowledge for teachers is that you should have a strong base *before* starting. Continue your learning. Question what you hear. Present your information as theory unless you have facts. Back up your speculation or facts with sources. Don't expect to know it all, but have resources you can quickly turn to for answers.

If you are a fusion instructor, this is doubly true for you. Many fusion or interpretive style dancers feel that they can do whatever they want and make things up as they go along. Everything -- even new styles -- is rooted in something. It's incredibly difficult to dance in a way that makes sense artistically, musically, and visually if it isn't first grounded in something that has already been identified. Fusion is so much harder to pull off than a dance that has been around for centuries and is well understood by audiences as well as performers. This is true because you have to really know where you came from before you can branch off in a meaningful way.

Costuming Knowledge

I've heard teachers tell their students, "Anything goes. Wear what you feel comfortable in." That is okay if you are performing interpretive dance and are labeling it as such. ("Interpretive dance" translates particular feelings and emotions, human conditions, situations, or fantasies into movement and dramatic expression. It can translate attributes of traditional movements into more modern expression.) That is not okay if you are doing Middle Eastern dance, a folkloric dance with its own history, culture, dress, and means of expression.

The problem is not one of personal expression. It's one of labeling. As an ambassador of a foreign art form, it's your responsibility to present it accurately. If you deviate from that, do it knowing that you are diverging from tradition and let your students know that as well. Deviate for a reason.

Costuming knowledge goes right along with cultural knowledge. If you can identify Dance A as Nubian, you should be able to tell your student what the appropriate costuming is for that dance. It's part of the job of being a teacher. "Wear whatever you want" is not an acceptable answer to a student's query of, "What should I wear?"

Stage make-up is part of costuming knowledge. If your students are going to be on stage, they have to know about stage make-up. This is NOT the same thing as street make-up. You would never see a ballet instructor let her 3- to 5-year-olds go on stage with street make-up or no make-up on. They learn what stage face looks like from their very first recital rehearsal. I am not sure why this isn't as common among belly dancers. What is true for them is more true for us. We are the pictures of fantasy. You can't be a fantasy if you look like your every day self.

I realize that stage make-up is an art unto itself, so it's not necessary that the instructor be able to teach it, but she should:

- have a contact to teach stage make-up if she can't
- be able to identify at a glance what's appropriate and what's not
- give quick tips on how to fix whatever is wrong

Application of stage make-up is another area where experts disagree. I've heard some experts recommend packing it on. Others go for a more natural look that achieves highlights and visibility through blending. Still others go for a middle ground that uses heavy make-up on some areas, color to achieve certain effects, and blending to create yet more effects.

As with gaining cultural and historical knowledge, this is something you are going to have to play with. Experiment with various techniques and see what gives you the best results. Be aware that lighting affects how the face looks and some techniques may work better in different environments than others. Again, the point is not to be a make-up expert, but to have enough knowledge that you can guide others. Why? Because this is a performing art. Being on stage in the appropriate costuming and make-up are part of it.

Musical Knowledge

Dance is the music made visible. Without knowledge of music, you cannot be a good dancer, much less a good teacher. Musical training will enhance *anyone's* ability to impart information in an understandable way. However, natural ability can also go a long way.

A teacher should know where to find the beat. She should be able to break the beat down into whole notes, half notes, quarter notes, eighth notes, and sixteenth notes and make that auditory to the student. She should be able to find the "one." She should be able to count and dance phrases of varying lengths, even if the music is syncopated. She should be able to double time or half time any move and stay on beat. These are very basic skills.

The music and dances of the Middle East are made up of rhythms that are very different from Western music. Before teaching a dance style of any region with particular rhythms attached to it, the teacher should know what those rhythms are and be able to clap, sing, or express them in an auditory way so that she can teach her students to follow them as well. If you can't hear the rhythm, you are likely to dance through it, and that's not really dancing to the music, is it? I am not saying that a teacher has to master *all* the rhythmic possibilities. That would take a lifetime. She should, however, be able to identify the ones she's dancing and teaching to.

A good teacher will know how to dance to *taxim,* an often nonrhythmic improvisation that is frequently done in live belly dance shows. There are going to be times when the music doesn't have a drum to follow. What happens then? A good teacher will be able to break down what to do there. Again, this is a basic belly dance skill.

Having knowledge of musical structure makes creating choreography so much easier because dance follows the flow of the music (or it *should!*) Knowing musical notation makes it easier to write choreographies as well. Musical training of any kind can greatly increase your effectiveness as a teacher.

I know that some people have differing views on the importance of finger cymbal playing, but I consider finger cymbal playing a basic belly dance skill. I think all teachers should know how to play a basic triple pattern on the *zils* while moving and teach their students to do the same. If you can play more intricate things, fine! You're ahead of the game, but I do believe that at a minimum, a teacher should be able to competently play *zils* while dancing. This is something that many students ask me to show them right off the bat. What kind of teacher would I be if I couldn't at least play a triple?

Basic Belly Dance Movement Knowledge

I know a lot of students start to teach because they outgrow their class and have nowhere else to go. They figure that if all they get are basics, and they've mastered those, they must be ready to teach. There is more to teaching than basic movements. You have to be able to transition them gracefully into other movements. You also have to know where to put them whether you are improvising or creating a choreography.

Creating dance is like creating a book. The basic movements are the words. The combinations are the sentences. The layers are the interesting things like suspense, theme, setting, and climax. The music and artistry bring it all together into a creative whole. Children don't go to first grade, learn how to print a few words, then strike out on their own to write a book. I am not sure why some dancers feel that they can do basically the same thing through dance. Not even all people who have mastered the art of writing sentences can write books.

There was a student in my area who had been to three teachers' beginning classes before coming to me. During class she would sigh, sit out, and stop participating. When I asked her what was up, she responded, "Why do we have to keep doing the same thing over and over?" A classmate piped up, "Because you don't have it yet!"

I told that student that she could test into the next level if she felt she knew it all, but instead she dropped out of the class and started her own class. I saw her perform for the first time not long after that. Not only could she not do basic movements in isolation, she also could not transition them. She did not have an understanding of the music, so she didn't know what went where.

I structure my classes in such a way that the student always has the opportunity to have a realistic appraisal of her skill level. Despite that, some people are going to do what they want to do and teach before they are ready. If you are reading this, I am comforted that you are concerned about not being one of them.

If you are not sure if you have mastered the basics, can use them in combinations and layers and know where to put them musically, technically, and artistically, ask someone you trust for an evaluation. Get some coaching or compete in a contest (they provide feedback on skills just like this). Do what it takes to get some objective feedback. You don't want to find out the hard way that you aren't ready.

How To Choreograph

When I started teaching, I had a very limited dance vocabulary and didn't know the first thing about choreography. My idea of creating choreography was to write down all the moves I knew. I'd pick one and do it for the length of a musical phrase, then go on to the next move and next musical phrase. I might throw in a few travel patterns for variety, but it was really pretty boring, unoriginal, and had nothing to do with the music. It got me through a song and gave me something to do but it was hardly dance.

I am sorry to say that I frequently see troupes performing the same type of stuff that I created when I first got started. That's not dance, folks. That's memorized moves in sequence. I get it. I did it too. I didn't have anyone to tell me differently. That's why I writing this for you.

I realize that it may be difficult to create beginner level choreography to use as a teaching tool to show how to transition moves and do simple layering. In order to create a choreography that uses the moves you want your students to know, it may feel a little like doing moves in sequence, but it should have *some* relationship to the music. It should show *some* awareness of space. If the music dictates that there is a mood change, the movements should reflect that. There should be a blend of the complex and simple. The routine should show a consideration for the number of dancers involved. In other words, it should be a dance rather than moves in sequence.

Keep in mind that choreography is a Western concept, so Western rules apply. It's a rather strange blend of East and West, but many students demand choreography. It's a convenient and effective teaching tool, so you can't get around it.

Unfortunately, there aren't a lot of belly dancers that understand the concepts of choreography, so there aren't many good examples to follow. If you don't have a grasp of what makes a good choreography, and don't have a reliable mentor to ask, check your local university for classes in choreography. You can also try these books:

Blom, Lynne Ann, T. Chaplin. *The Intimate Act of Choreography*. University of Pittsburgh Press, 1982.

Burrows, Jonathan. *A Choreographer's Handbook*. Routledge, 2010.

Cerny Minton, Sandra. *Choreography: A Basic Approach Using Improvisation -3rd Edition.* Human Kinetics, 2007.

Ellfeldt, Lois. *A Primer for Choreographers.* Waveland Press, Inc., 1988.

Humphrey, Doris. *The Art of Making Dances.* Princeton Book Company, 1991.

Kaplan, Robert. *Rhythmic Training for Dancers.* Human Kinetics. 2002.

Koner, Paula. *Elements of Performance: A Guide for Performers in Dance, Theatre and Opera.* Routledge, 1993.

The books aren't specific to Middle Eastern dance, but the concepts still apply. Some target one area more than others, so check out a few references to get a holistic understanding.

How to Improvise

Students generally fall into two camps, those who want structure from start to finish, and those who like to improvise. As a teacher you have to be able to do both. Improvisation is not just a free style performance. In order for it to be dance, it has to have a relationship to the music. That's the element I most often find lacking in the improvisation I see. Many dancers can go out there and dance their hearts out. They are full of energy and passion, but there is no connection to the music and no structure.

In order to improvise well, you must understand how music is constructed. I promise you, it's not random. Music follows certain predictable patterns. If you are intuitively aware of what those patterns are, you can improvise and hit the accents and changes even if you've never heard the song before.

Good improvisation also relies on a strong dance vocabulary. It's not enough to know the basics in isolation, you have to have programmed in your muscle memory combinations and layers so that they easily flow from you just at the right time. Even though improvisation means "unrehearsed," you have to rehearse the elements of the dance over and over in order for it to be there when you reach for it.

If you understand what I am saying and can execute that, you still have to be able to explain that to your students. "Follow the leader" is not enough. It may help the moves to flow, but you're relying on hit and miss in order for the concept to sink in. If you have a bunch of students who resist improvisation because there is no set right or wrong, it will be difficult to teach this. You have to have their trust. You have to give them a framework to hang onto. They need specific, concrete instruction on what to do differently in order to progress. It's not easy for some people to let go and just fly.

Knowledge of Body Mechanics

Every student is responsible for her own safety. The teacher cannot adapt every movement in every class to one person's injuries, illness, disease, or poor habits, but a good teacher will have enough knowledge of body mechanics always to demonstrate safe technique.

The teacher should have an awareness of how to conduct proper warm-ups before beginning class. While belly dance is generally considered safe and gentle, each student's level of fitness may affect her ability to do movements correctly. The best precaution against muscle tearing is a proper warm-up. A proper warm-up increases body temperature, muscle elasticity, and blood flow. It helps to focus the mind on the dance. Injuries also can be caused by poor posture, body misalignment, and incorrect technique. All these issues should be caught by a vigilant teacher's eye. The teacher should know how to correct the problem and teach the student to spot misalignment and to fix it on her own.

Body mechanics is another area where there is a lot of conflicting information. I've studied with many well-known instructors who wanted to guide me to painful and incorrect body movements. It's incredibly important, for your health and the health of your students, that *you* know what's safe and what's not. While I recommend cross training, I caution against bringing in knowledge from one discipline and applying it to belly dance. I can tell you that that may not work. However, if you want to cross train, the best cross training program I can recommend is Alexander Technique or The Feldekrais Method.

Teaching Skills

Knowledge of dance is not enough to make you a teacher. You also have to have the ability to impart information in a variety of ways. People learn differently. If you teach with only one method, you are not going to reach the people who do not learn effectively with your style.

Every teacher will have her own way of doing things. What works for each person is partially personality driven, but some skills common to good teachers are the ability to teach in different ways, stay focused on one thing at a time, teach in spirals, and involve the students in the teaching process.

Most people have the ability to see, hear, touch, feel and sense things. Most of us also process information primarily through one system, then through the others. In the USA, most of us are visual. That's great for the teacher with the "follow-me" teaching system. That's not great for the student who is primarily auditory or kinesthetic.

The auditory student is one who processes information through sound first. The kinesthetic student primarily processes information through feeling first.

If a student is having a hard time grasping a topic, that's a hint that the student's primary information processing system is not the one that you are using to send information. It's up to you to adapt to her lead system so that she can get the material. In other words, explain the concepts in different ways so that everyone can understand. The most effective way to teach is to consistently use all three modalities simultaneously.

You can easily tell which system a person is using by paying attention to what they say.

Visual people use phrases that indicate that they process information through their eyes:

1. I **see** what you mean.
2. I can visualize it.
3. That **looks** good to me.
4. I drew a **blank**.
5. Give me time to **focus** on that.

Auditory people use phrases that convey sound, such as:

6. I **hear** what you are saying.
7. That **sounds** great to me!
8. Now that's an **earful**.
9. That **rings** a bell.
10. I know I've **heard** that before.
11. Listen to me.
12. Let's **talk**.

Kinesthetic people speak in touching and feeling phrases including:

13. How does that **feel** to you?
14. Let me get a **handle** on that.
15. This is really hard for me to **grasp**.
16. I need to **tackle** this job.

There are other methods to tell which lead system people are using. There are other ways to connect with people in order to communicate more effectively. If you are interested in learning them, check out resources on neuro-linguistic programming (NLP).

If you have a lesson plan you should have no problem staying on target, but I've visited several classrooms where there was no rhyme or reason to what was going on that day. There was a little bit of this and a little bit of that. Students can't learn if you don't stay focused on a single topic long enough for them to digest the material.

Having a lesson plan does not guarantee that you will stay on track. Something may come up to sidetrack the class. That's okay if the diversion was worth exploring, but make sure that you come back to what you were planning.

"Teaching in spirals" basically means building on past lessons to strengthen past learning and connect new learning to an old concept. A good lesson plan should always lead in spirals. This should be fairly easy as the concepts in dance always overlap. When you do this intentionally, your students get a reinforcing effect.

There are many ways to involve the students in the teaching process. In my intermediate class, we watch videos of various styles we are studying, and then I ask the students to comment on what they saw. I am looking for their thought process. Did they see that this dancer was not connecting to the audience? Did they notice that another one had on a costume that was not appropriate for the styles of dance? Did they think this one was technically proficient? Knowing that I am going to ask questions forces them to pay attention. Their comments tell me how much they are absorbing and if they are on track.

I also have my intermediate level students give each other feedback on their homework assignments. The atmosphere is constructive and safe, otherwise I would not encourage this, but this practice helps them to develop a critical eye. They begin to understand what works, what doesn't, and why. They have feedback from more than one person, so they begin also to understand that feedback on dance is somewhat subjective. What appeals to one person may not be attractive to another. This teaches them to let the subjective stuff roll off their backs.

Involving the student in the teaching process is a great help to teachers because it gives instant feedback on what the student is thinking and absorbing. It helps the teacher to see the thought process. It's a fantastic feedback tool to let the teacher know if an idea was conveyed successfully.

Working with Props

I don't consider proficiency with props a "must have" skill for teachers, but teachers should have at least a passing familiarity with props. Most students want to learn how to dance with a veil. Many like sword. Some students go prop crazy and get into wild prop configurations like sword and veil, double veil, poi balls, feather fans, flaming hoops, and belly beads. You should be able to at least give some introductory information on props and get your students started on the path to discovery.

If props are not your cup of tea, don't worry. You don't have to be able to juggle flaming swords in order to be a good teacher. You should know a reputable source for your students to go to, though. Part of what makes a good teacher "good" is that she knows her limitations and will refer to others when needed.

Willingness to Continue Training

As you might imagine, it's difficult to keep up on all the skills required to be a good teacher. The learning process never stops. A good teacher must be willing to continue her own training. Training includes dance classes, instruction on how to teach, studying history and culture, and cross training in areas like music, Tai Chi, Pilates, or Alexander Technique.

You are never going to know it all, but everything you learn increases your ability to share. It makes you a more valuable part of the community. It can increase the price that you command because *you* become an expert! Learning more is a no-lose proposition. In fact, it's essential to being and remaining a good teacher.

You can easily spot teachers who don't continue their training. They may look like they are stuck in a time warp, doing a style of dance that was popular way back when. They may use the same routines over and over for years. They may say things like they invented belly dance, are the only authentic dancer around, or that no one is better than they are so why bother training with someone else.

It's true that the more advanced you become, the harder it is to find classes geared to your skill and interest level, but you can always take private lessons or learn more about a style of dance that you are not proficient in. There is no good reason to stop training as long as you are teaching.

Are You Ready?

Here is a check list of skills dancers should have before they begin teaching. Check off the items that you already have. If the ones you don't have aren't critical, go ahead and start your class and work on getting what you currently lack. If you are missing necessary basic skills, get the training or knowledge you need *before* taking people's money for lessons. It will give you a stronger start when you do begin teaching and make you more confident.

____ discipline

____ flexibility

____ can balance praise with constructive criticism

____ can control the learning environment

____ cultural knowledge

____ historical knowledge

____ costuming knowledge

____ make-up knowledge

____ musical knowledge

____ can play and teach basic zils

____ can execute and teach basic steps, combinations, layers

____ knows where to put basic steps, combinations, layers

____ knows how to choreograph

____ knows how to improvise

____ has a basic understanding of healthy posture and body alignment

____ has solid basic teaching skills

____ can work with props

____ has a willingness to continue training

The point of the list isn't to discourage you from getting started, but to give you a realistic appraisal of where you are and to get you where you want to be. Honest self-critique is your friend!

Here's one final checklist to help you decide if you are ready: Maslow's Stages of Learning. The stages are Unconscious Incompetence, Conscious Incompetence, Conscious Competence, and Unconscious Competence.

Unconscious Incompetence is when you don't know what you don't know. This could describe someone who isn't even taking dance lessons yet, an audience member, a beginner, or someone who has taken dance lessons for many years. It's not about the amount of exposure to dance someone has, but about having the intellectual knowledge to know what the dancer is doing, if she's doing it well, why she's doing it the way she's doing it, and if something is wrong, knowing how to fix it. In other words, the person in the Unconscious Incompetence stage doesn't know that there is more to know. She only knows what she likes and how things feel.

I once took a group of students to a show. We had a thirteen year old girl there who had been dancing about 3 months. She was cute as could be. She had no fear and went out there and worked the crowd. Later the host told me she was the best performer of the night. Knowing her skill level and that of the other performers, I knew that was certainly not true.

She may have been the most entertaining to the host, but the host was operating at the Unconscious Incompetence level. It's great for us as performers when our audience is ignorant because they are easier to please, but it's not good for the student to rely on praise and crowd pleasing to measure her skill. If my student accepted the host's comments as fact, she may have quit taking lessons, started dancing professionally or started teaching at her low level because she also was at a stage where she didn't that there was more to know.

Ignorance is not a crime. It's just what we experience when we are doing something new. Like all people, I went through this stage. When I was a new dancer, I was at a video party watching a highly skilled dancer with boredom. I didn't like her style, so I dismissed her as being someone I didn't want to learn from. The more experienced dancers didn't say anything, but I could tell they thought I was insane.

Looking back, I laugh at how ignorant I was. Regardless of whether I liked her style, I couldn't appreciate the dancer's skill because I didn't have it and didn't know what it would take to get it!

Many instructors start teaching at this stage. I was one of them. Since they don't know what they don't know, it seems perfectly logical to start teaching because there is nothing holding them back. If this is you, don't worry. There is no shame in being a neophyte. We all start somewhere. The goal now is to move beyond your ignorance.

If we stick with something long enough, have a good teacher, and practice mindfully, we get to the next stage, which is Conscious Incompetence. This is where the light bulb comes on and we get a clue that there is more to learn. This can be emotionally overwhelming as we think things like, "I will never catch up. How will I afford the classes I need? Will I have time to devote to this? I have no business being out there dancing in front of people!"

A lot of people give up at this stage. Their anxiety gets the best of them, but this is just a normal part of learning. This is the point at which real progress can be made because you are starting to know enough about what you are doing to know when it's good and when it's bad. This is an information gathering stage. You may sort what you want from what you don't want. There are lots of fits and starts that take you to the next stage.

When I started formulating goals for my students, and myself I started realizing all the things that they and I did not know. That helped me tremendously because it gave me focus to start getting what I didn't have. So, this stage can be motivating or debilitating. It's really up to you. Either course is normal, but why not choose the more constructive path?

The Conscious Competence stage is the working stage. You know what you need to know. You can do what you have to do, but you have to think about it to do it proficiently. The struggle is gone, but effort is still required. It's here that you start to see results that can propel you to the next stage.

Conscious Incompetence is the stage we all strive for. This is where you can do something effortlessly without thinking about it. Of course that move was technically flawless, musical, and emotionally effective! You've done it so many times in so many ways that it just arrives without thought.

It's normal to be at various levels of learning with different skills. Perhaps your business acumen is flawless while you are still developing your instructor skills. Or maybe you can teach beginners classes at a Conscious Competent level but your mixed level workshop skills are Conscious Incompetence level. That's okay. It's all about using the knowledge you have to move beyond your present limitations.

Maslow's stages of learning stopped at level four. Many feel that there is a fifth level. I agree. Some say it has to do with being mindful. Others, like me, say that it has to do with being able to articulate, explain, and/or teach that knowledge to others. At this stage you not only know something, you can do it flawlessly over and over and can show others how to do it too. When you see an error in the execution, you can point out the flaw and tell someone how to fix it. Good performers must get to the fourth level. Excellent instructors must achieve the fifth.

Obviously the ideal way to do it is to wait until you reach level five to begin teaching, but we can't always wait for what is ideal. Use your best judgment and move forward.

TAAJ

DOES IT MAKE SENSE TO TEACH?

Many people start teaching because that's the next destination on the path they are on. Don't let that be your reason for teaching. It's a very inefficient way to make life choices. Instead I urge you to ask yourself, "Is teaching the best way to reach my goals?"

To answer this question, you have to know your why. What is it that you want to get out of teaching? What I mean is, what emotional need will you fulfill by teaching?

Most human motivations fit into one of six categories: safety/security; variety/adventure; significance; connection; growth; contribution. Everyone needs all these things to feel whole; however, we generally have one or two that trump all the others. If we have these, we feel happy. When we find the thing that gives us all six, we have found our passion!

Safety/security is a sense of certainty or stability. It is knowing that you can count on things to be a predictable way. It is about trust and keeping things the same.

Variety/adventure is just the opposite. This is a need for newness, novelty, and stimulation. It is wanting to shake things up. It is spontaneity, energy, and life. It's about doing and experiencing for its own sake.

Significance is about feeling important, valued, or special. It is a need to know that you are appreciated and have meaning.

Connection is about intimacy. It is a feeling of "we" vs. "me." It's about sisterhood, community, and shared experiences.

Growth is about expanding your mind. New ideas and experiences are had for the purpose of learning and being more than you are now.

Contribution is about giving. This one can sometimes look like other needs. If you learn things in order to share with others, your emotional need may be to contribute rather than to grow. If you spend time with others to give to them rather than to feel a sense of connection, your emotional need may be to contribute.

There are effective and ineffective ways to get our needs met. Below are some examples.

	Effective	Ineffective
Safety/security	Work regularly; save; delay gratification; express discipline; stick to a schedule; get a degree in a stable field; avoid risks; perform choreographies; plan everything; stick to what you are good at; dress conservatively; follow the rules;	Work at a job you don't like; stick to a behavior, relationship, or belief that doesn't serve you; test other people's boundaries; avoid risks;
Variety/adventure	Sky dive; explore multiple careers; travel; eat unfamiliar foods; learn new things; ride roller coasters; dance improvisationally	Make impulsive decisions; frequently change jobs, partners or friends; engage in risky or dangerous behaviors; lie; break the rules

Significance	Invest in unique cars, clothes, friends or activities; attain status; have a wealthy, beautiful or successful spouse; be on stage; live a high-profile life	Push kids or spouse to be successful; engage in attention-getting behaviors such as depression, exhibitionism, physical illness, hysterics, sex with strangers; commit crimes; display explosive anger
Connection	Social activities; romantic relationships; host parties; have a pen pal; lunch with a friend	Have sex with inappropriate people; give too much, accept abuse; fight
Growth	Take a class; learn something new; teach; read; play games; spend time in observation	Provoke trouble (civilly, socially, etc.)
Contribution	Write; create things; donate; volunteer; teach; give money	Tell people what to do; do other people's work for them

Understanding your "why" can help you to see if you are meeting your needs in an effective way. For example, if teaching is a way to meet your need for connection, and connection is low on your list of needs, perhaps teaching is not really all that important. On the other hand, if teaching meets four of your emotional needs, it probably feels like something that you must do.

TAAJ

PAVING YOUR WAY TO SUCCESS

What is Your Goal?

I started teaching because I felt it was expected. I had a willing audience. I didn't see a good reason to say no. I spent the next five years foundering, doing a little of this and that, until I stumbled into my purpose. I could have saved myself a lot of time and trial and error had I simply asked the question, "What do I want to get out of this?" The answer to that question is your goal. Always start with your goal *and then* figure out the means to get there.

Defining my goal, or my why, was a game changer. I was having fun before, but it often felt like work. If I felt fulfilled at the end of the day, that was a lucky byproduct. It wasn't planned. Once I knew what I wanted to get out of teaching, my teaching became not only more purposeful, but more effective. By saying no to the things that took me away from my goals and yes to the things that enhanced my goals made my business more fulfilling and profitable.

Some goals could be:

I want this to pass along my knowledge to other dancers. (contribution)

I want to create many big name dancers/have a legacy. (significance)

I want to share my love of dance with other people. (connection, contribution)

I want to have a group of dancers to perform with. (connection)

I want to have an outlet for my creativity. (variety, growth)

I want to make money. (security)

I want to have a way to finance my dance education and performances. (security)

I want the dance history and culture to live on after me. (contribution)

I want to keep learning and growing in the dance. (growth)

I want to have back-up dancers for my feature performances. (significance)

I want to have students who idolize me. (significance)

I want to create a name for myself. (significance)

Don't be afraid to state what you want. There is no shame in being ambitious, wanting to make money, or to be successful. If you can't state your goals, you'll have a hard time meeting them, so just be honest. Say it.

Now that you know what your personal goals are, it's time to define your goal for your class. If there is more than one class, you will have a goal for each one. If you have a different goal for the school, be sure to state that too. All these things, combined with your why, will help you to see when things are out of alignment. Having all aspects of your business working in the same direction creates a streamline effect that makes things go more smoothly.

Some examples of class goals could be:

Students will have fun while learning basic belly dance skills.

Students will be able to perform a basic choreography.

Students will reinforce muscle memory through drills.

Students will be able to play a triple pattern while dancing.

Students will increase their combination repertoire.

Now let's check to see if everything is working in alignment. Let's say your why, or most important emotional needs, are variety and connection. Your personal goal is to have an outlet for your creativity, and your class goal is to for students to be able to perform a basic choreography. All those things are in alignment. If your why is growth and significance, your personal goal is to create a name for yourself, and your class goal is for students to play a triple pattern while dancing, that may not be the most fulfilling plan unless it is a stepping stone to grander things.

We all suffer from burn-out. We all have periods when our work doesn't have the juice that it used to or that we want it to. Usually it is because things have gone out of alignment. It's a good idea to review your whys and goals regularly to see if they are still appropriate. After all, once you achieve a goal, it could be time to set another one as you grow with each accomplishment.

Even if you are someone who needs safety and stability, don't stick with the same game plan year after year. Find a way to have some things stay the same while others are changing. Why? Because a person or business that is not growing is dying. The world is always in flux. Look at music, costume, and style trends. What worked in the '90s is vintage now. If you don't evolve, you will eventually look like a dinosaur and have a hard time attracting new students.

I am not saying that you can't love your style and teach old school material. After all I am not the only one who still loves Samia and Nadia Gamal. I am just saying that you may want to incorporate other styles, new ways of teaching, or do something more innovative than simply creating new choreographies to keep you and your students inspired and growing.

Using Your Why to Create Your How

As you can see in the chart above, there are many ways to get your needs met. Some are effective. Some are ineffective. (Note that "effective" means that your strategies not only meet your needs, but do so in a way that creates no negative repercussions for yourself, other people, or other areas of your life.) When you use your why to create your how, you are more likely to craft a plan that will make you happy and reach your goals.

You will have lots of decisions to make about what to do, what not to do, and how to do it. It's sometimes easy to go with the flow and say yes to whatever comes your way. It's easy to look at someone else's path and simply follow in their footsteps. Those are not the best ways to have a successful business because everyone is different. As you lay down your plans and reach new crossroads, ask yourself, "What is my *why*?" and you will find clarity.

For example, let's say that "Hadia" and "Badia" have the opportunity to dance at a charity event with an expected attendance of one thousand people and no pay. Hadia's top two emotional needs are connection and significance. The rest of her emotional needs are either well met or are unimportant. She is a teacher who could use more students. She hopes that this event will expose her to people who will hire her. She also feels a lot of connection and significance when dancing. So this could be an opportunity that she says yes to because it could meet her goal of introducing her to potential clients and her emotional needs will be met.

Badia's top two needs, on the other hand, are safety and growth. She would also welcome more students. She meets her need for growth through teaching so she feels pretty full. She feels best when her work produces money (safety). As this performance job may not produce any money at all and will not likely impact her desire for growth, Badia may not feel like this is much of an opportunity at all. So, this "how" is not a great way to meet Badia's "why."

Not all our needs will be met through dance. If dance takes away from another job (safety), a love relationship (connection), a hobby (adventure), or some other need, it may not be a good trade. Remember to balance your life so that you have more than one way to meet your needs. Things happen. If you suddenly lose a big chunk of your life, it's easy to feel as if you have lost your balance, your identity, or your reason for being. If you spread out your risk so that no one thing has enough power to upset the entire apple cart, you will always have more flexibility and less vulnerability.

TAAJ

GETTING STARTED

The Plan

Starting a new endeavor requires a plan. Your plan should address what you will teach, where you will teach, what your expenses will be, and what exactly you are willing to do. After that we'll look at pricing. These are interrelated and should be considered together.

What You Will Teach

If you are like most people, there is a particular style of dance that speaks to you. You haven't really thought about teaching anything else. You want to teach *that* because you love *that*.

If you think about the most popular teachers out now, you can create a picture in your mind of what their signature look is like, what type of music they use, and what style they do, right? That is what you want to cultivate as well. When people think of you, they should have one unifying vision in mind. That unifying vision is your niche.

If you are like me and Variety rates high on your list, you may have the problem of wanting to do lots of things. In that case, your "What" may not be about what style of dance to teach but something broader. My "What" evolved into teaching people to grow into their own style and be the best dancer that they could be. Another broad niche could be creating huge fantasy spectacles or keeping vintage choreographies alive.

One thing to consider when settling on your what is the marketplace. If the market doesn't support your vision, you will either have to tweak it so that does, abandon your ideas, or add something to the mix that will bring in the money to allow you to also do what you love. For example, it may be acceptable to you to teach a bellyrobics class for twenty people to support the class that you love that only has four students.

Which of those options to choose isn't about what you *should* do. It's about what would be the most effective thing for your lifestyle, your values, and your goals. Don't forget to consider your Why to see what makes most sense for you.

Where You Will Teach

The typical choices for where to teach, and the ones I'd recommend if you are just starting out, are the home studio, a rented studio, or teaching for hire. The home studio is attractive because it's usually the cheapest and most convenient option. There are start-up costs for each option, but little additional monthly overhead expenses with the home studio. This can mean it is the most lucrative option.

Let's look at my teaching path as an example. Here is a look at my emotional needs to help make sense of things.

16 % ■
connection

10 % ■
significance

5 % ■
safety

19 % ■
adventure

28 % ■
growth

22 % ■
contribution

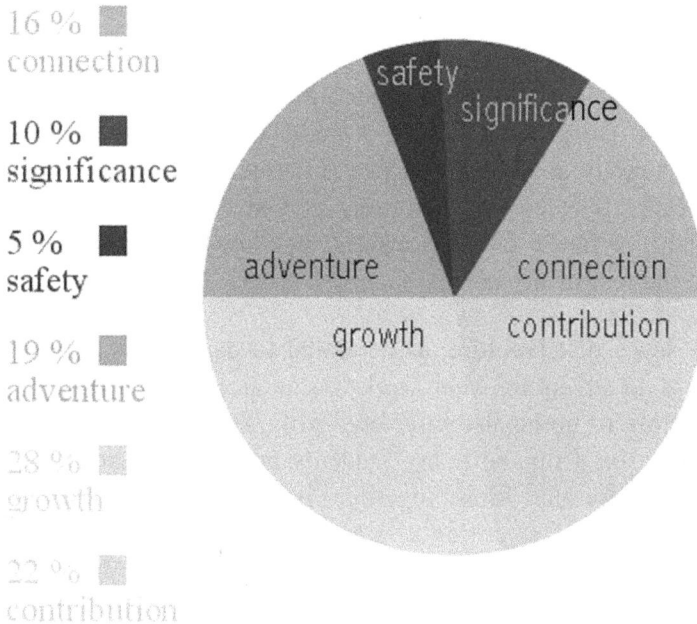

I started out teaching out of my den. There was no furniture in it, so there was plenty of space. There was an entrance just off to the side, so students didn't have to come through the rest of my house or disrupt anything else that was going on with the family. For a while it seemed like an ideal plan.

After a while, my husband started complaining that he had nowhere to park. Even though we were in a room closed off by a door, he felt like he couldn't relax until after everyone was gone. He felt that our home was being invaded.

Over time, I also began to feel like I never left work. At that time, I was a full-time performer, troupe director, teacher, and importer. Everywhere I looked there was something work related to do. Costumes were here. Merchandise was there. The home phone was also my work phone. I woke up feeling like I was at work. I went to sleep feeling like I was at work. There was no escape. Little by little, the home studio began to seem like a really bad idea.

Now let's look back and see why this could have been really predictable and avoided. Since my top two needs are contribution and growth, having a studio in my home could look like a really good idea as dance is a way that I meet both those needs. It keeps my business and students close and convenient. What I didn't consider was how that decision affected the rest of my pie.

My sense of adventure, as it related to dance, was gone. There was no adventure when work was all around me. Having work so close to home also interfered with my romantic life. I got connection from both my students and my spouse, but when they were that close together, it felt as if they were competing for my attention. I was still getting growth and contribution, but as you can see they are already overwhelming my pie. Now they took over and were squeezing everything out so my life became very unbalanced.

So, my next move was to teach in a studio. The studio seemed like a fabulous move! It was $200 per month for three hours a week.

There were no utility payments or taxes. It was bigger, brighter, and had mirrors. The studio was inside an alternative therapy physical rehabilitation center. That was a boon to business as many of those clients were eager to try belly dance as a gentle form of exercise. Unfortunately, many also had physical limitations so I was stuck with the choice of losing them or modifying the class. I tried both options and ultimately let the physical therapy patients go. I was really there to teach dance. At that time, I was not qualified to do dance as therapy, so there wasn't really any choice.

When I lost the flow of students from the center, I really had to focus on attracting new students. When I was in my house, it didn't matter. I had no overhead. Here it mattered a lot! That added quite a bit of work and expense that I didn't have before.

After the honeymoon phase was over, I began to feel like a stepchild at the center. Our space was sometimes crowded with stuff from the center, so all the space was not available. Sometimes I was told the space wouldn't be available on our regularly scheduled day because of something going on at the center. Other little things happened that seemed to send the message of, "This is my space and you're just using it. If I need it for something, you will just have to adjust." I felt restricted which killed my sense of adventure. In the end, I didn't like using someone else's space very much. There were too many restrictions and inconveniences.

I could have predicted this by looking at my pie. While adventure comes in third on my chart, it still ranks a whooping 19%. When my sense of adventure goes, things aren't fun anymore. Since I am a hard charger and work at growth, both for my students, and myself it really has to be fun in order to keep me going. After all, all work and no play makes Jill a dull girl. So even though only one aspect of my emotional needs was really impacted by moving into the studio, draining my sense of adventure made a big, negative difference in my overall satisfaction and productivity.

Working in someone else's space doesn't have to be horrible. I have worked in a fitness center as an employee where all I had to do was show up, do my thing, and leave. No dragging equipment in and out, no cleaning up after anyone, no taking phone calls or signing anyone up. That was easy! But it also paid peanuts. I don't have a high need for safety/money, but my need for significance is twice that of my safety. I would not respect myself if I felt I was giving away my hard won talent, so this wasn't a viable option for me long term.

I worked in an alternative health clinic as a dance teacher for hire. I worked for a split of the tuition, so the pay was good. I was there after everyone else was gone, so I had the run of the place. Again, it was pretty easy. No equipment to drag in. No phone calls to answer. No rent to pay. The downside was that I never knew how many students I would have for class because the center was doing the promotion. Some days it was bursting through the walls. Other days there might only be one or two students. If I were relying on that money for income, I would have had to quit. It was too unpredictable. This might be okay for someone with a high sense of adventure, but it wasn't a good way to meet my needs for growth and contribution because there was no way to move the class forward when there were never the same people in class.

I relate my experience in the different environments to give you an idea of what considerations you might face. Everyone will have different factors that will influence choice. There is a definite loss of privacy when using your home as your studio. There can be no sense of freedom or flexibility when you rent space from someone else. Working for someone else can be unpredictable because you're relying on them to do the advertising and getting the students in. It's great if they do their part, but not so great if they don't. Of course you can and should do promotion too.

The positive side to all these options is that you have little invested if you decide you don't want to teach after all or if you don't get the business you had hoped for. You can walk away fairly easily with little damage done. It's a great way to test the waters.

I wouldn't think too hard on this. It can lead to paralysis by analysis. If you think you have a good plan that feels good, go back to your why and do a best guess as to whether you think it will work for you. Try it out and revise as needed using your knowledge of your why to make your next plan more effective.

What You Are Willing to Do

Belly dance is one of the few dance genres that expects the instructor to be a good teacher, performer, choreographer, troupe director, costume designer, marketer, seamstress, and so many other things. Few people have the talent or desire to do all those things well, yet here we are.

A good game plan is to decide in advance what you are willing to do and how much time you are willing to spend doing it. Belly dance can easily take over your life otherwise.

Ask yourself what are you capable of doing, what do you want to do, and what do you have time to do. That should whittle down your list of responsibilities to a manageable level. If you are a belly dancing super woman who has the time and ability to do all those things, you may go back to "what is my Why?" If sewing costumes doesn't meet your needs, that may be all you need to know to cut it from your list of responsibilities.

Some of us are one trick ponies – either by knowledge, skill, time, or desire. If this is you, don't sell yourself short. Knowing your limitations is essential to crafting a good game plan. Don't be tempted to go beyond your limitations to compete. You can have a more satisfying and successful business doing what you know well than doing a wide variety of things with mediocrity. If you say no with purpose, it's easier to feel good about saying no.

Don't forget that you can always hire someone to do what you don't want to do if you feel it is essential. If you have advanced level students, you can recruit them to help as well. When I had a troupe, we had a music and costume lieutenant. Many had come from classes where they had no input, so they were happy to help. It gave them a sense of ownership and pride in our productions and made them feel like valuable and honored members of the team. I still had the final say. Delegating those responsibilities to competent people took a lot of work off my back that I didn't want to do and created a win/win situation for the group.

Here's a sample diagram that may help you draw appropriate boundaries.

"Nadia's" whys are connection and significance

	Time	Why?	Interest	Skill
Choreography	Yes	Yes, both	High	Moderate
Troupe director	No	Yes, both	Low	Low to moderate
Recitals	Yes	Yes, both	Moderate	High
Costume designer	No	Significance if done well	Low	Low
Seamstress	Yes	No	No	High
Performer	Yes	Yes, both	High	High
Workshop sponsor	No	Yes, both	Moderate	Low to moderate
Vendor	No	No	Moderate	High

Based on the chart above, it looks like Nadia's best chance at having a fulfilling business would be to limit work responsibilities to choreography, recitals, and her own performances.

Pricing

Most people set their price based upon what others are charging. This is not a viable strategy if you want to be profitable. After all, you don't want it costing you to teach!

In order to set a fair wage, you have to know what your expenses are. This might sound obvious, but think about it. If you are making minimum wage to teach at a recreation center and it costs you more in gas money and babysitting than you are making, you are paying to teach. Always consider your costs.

To determine your cost of doing business, add up *all* costs. Costs include things like rent, insurance, taxes, advertising, interest on loans, depreciation, wages, commissions, utilities, postage, continued training, costuming, music, make-up, transportation, and office supplies. The total of all these costs will be your break even point. If you make just enough to cover costs, you will have no income.

Now let's calculate your cost per hour. It's difficult to determine how much it costs you to produce a service, but here is the formula.

Expenses + (mark-up percentage of expenses) gives you the amount you need to make each month.

Let's say that teaching is a part-time source of income and your total monthly business expenses are $300. Your work consumes twenty hours each month (this includes rehearsal, teaching classes, driving to the job, preparing music, acquiring costuming, taxes, and music, etc.) Your formula looks like this: 300 (expenses) + 900 (300% of $300) = $1200 per month. If you have four classroom hours per month, you divide $1200 by four, which is $300. So you need to price your classes so that you gross $300 per class. If you average ten students, that's $30 per student per class. I wouldn't price lower than that because you don't want to stress yourself out with maintaining larger classes. If you have more students than this in each class, consider it gravy.

You might ask, "Why did you set your mark-up so high?" Because belly dance is the type of business with wild fluctuations in supply and demand. You have to cover for slow periods and other things that don't generate income. Perhaps 300% is not high enough!

Assess the current market value of your service and adjust accordingly.

If market research shows that consumers won't pay the price determined by the formula, you either have to reduce your mark-up, cut costs, sell more, streamline the time it takes to produce a product or service or choose another business. If your market research determines that the value is higher than the price indicated by the formula, charge more! The formula is just a starting point. There are other factors that influence where to go from there.

Consider where you are in the price scale. Look at your competition. Are you a Benz or a Chevy? If you are appealing to the budget conscious, don't start with your price too low. You don't want to undercut the market. You also want to allow wiggle room so that you can cut prices if there is a downturn in the economy or there is suddenly fierce competition for budget business.

There is room for Wal-Mart and Nordstrom in the same town. If you are going for a high-end clientele, be sure to provide the quality that a high price demands. If the service does not live up to customer expectation, you will not be in business long. People are much more forgiving if you price low and disappoint. If your service is comparable to what others can offer, your price should be in the same range.

What's a Chevy price and a Benz price for your area? You can hire someone to do market research for you or do some informal research by checking out what similar businesses are charging. What does a singing telegram go for? A stripper? A clown? Other dance classes, dance gear, or performances?

If you can live on the income generated from your product or sales and the number of hours required to generate that income is acceptable to you, you have created a winning pricing formula.

Before I leave the subject of pricing, I feel compelled to address the prevalent attitude of "I charge $0-$5 per class because belly dance should be accessible to everybody." My first class was $10. That was in 1995. Guess what some people are charging for classes today? You guessed it, $10. Some are even less.

When you're unwilling to charge a living wage, you diminish the value of the dance. You make it harder for those who want to dance and teach full-time to get there because they can't be fairly compensated for it. It may create short-term happiness for you while creating depressed wages on a large scale. If you must decrease prices, please consider doing it on a case-by-case basis. I just checked the website of a local entry level ballet studio (meaning they cater to 3- to 5-year-olds with no previous experience). They are charging $135 per month for four hours of instruction. If parents are willing to pay that for a toddler, adults can pay more than $10 for their own classes.

TAAJ

KEEP MOVING

Once you have a plan for getting started, your work isn't done! Having a plan for how to keep moving forward is essential for planned growth. Your work, profit, and satisfaction level should be evaluated regularly to be sure that things continue to function well. Don't worry. This part isn't at all difficult. It just requires a few basic elements. If you keep these in mind and make them a habit, you will spend more time doing what you love while the little things take care of themselves.

Commit to a Growth Mindset

There is one essential skill that is required for all the rest to work. That is a growth mindset. (See *Mindset; The New Psychology of Success* by Carol Dweck for an in depth look at mindset). You can financially succeed without one. You can become well known without one, but the ride is easier and a lot more enjoyable with one. So why embrace the growth mindset?

Here is a chart that illustrates the contrasts between a growth mindset and its opposite, the fixed mindset.

Fixed Mindset	Growth Mindset
Sees things like talent and intelligence as something you are born with.	Sees things like talent and intelligence as something that can be developed.
Thinks that things should be easy so effort is avoided, as talent is everything.	Sees effort as a way to grow and achieve. Any skill can be developed.
Avoids challenges to keep from showing others what they don't know.	Embraces challenges because they are seen as a tool for self development.
Gives up easily to avoid showing others their shortcomings.	Persists, believing that mistakes are a part of life and answers are forthcoming.
Avoids or ignores negative feedback.	Uses negative feedback as a tool for growth.
Feels diminished by others' success.	Is fueled by others' success. If one can do it, others can too.
Feels life is predetermined by Fate or genes.	Feels empowered to make life whatever she wants it to be.
Sees failure as a reflection of who she is as a person.	Sees failure as a learning opportunity.
Focuses on results.	Focuses on the process.
Is risk averse.	Takes calculated risks.
Repeats what she is good at.	Tends to keep evolving.
Sees setbacks as catastrophic.	Sees setbacks as temporary.
Tends to isolate and be protective. "This is mine!"	Tends to be more open and sharing. "There's more where this came from."

If you were a gifted prodigy or a slow learner, you are more likely to have a fixed mindset because you probably got a lot of messages early on teaching you that you either were or weren't going to be a brain surgeon, astronaut, brilliant dancer, or superhero. Whether you believed you were talented or not, you probably didn't try too hard. Why would you when you were being told that your future was already mapped out for you?

The good news is, mindset is learned. It's not too late to start developing your skills right now. Instead of saying, "I can't ..." turn it into "I haven't yet learned to ..." Then apply the necessary skill until you can do whatever it is you want to do. Treat everything as a learning opportunity and it will be. There can be no failure unless you give up trying. Just stay in the game and enjoy the process and you will find that you have developed a growth mindset. The rest of the skills will talk about this in more detail.

Commit to Constant Improvement

The Belly Dance Trainer (BDT) certification program is all about constant improvement. It sets out to give the teacher a basic template for success then challenges them to keep improving upon it. Why? Because nothing is ever as good as it gets. Even if you have stratospheric success, you can always go higher. If that type of growth is possible, why not achieve it for yourself, your students, and your studio?

This attitude is illustrated by the Japanese concept of Kaizen. There is no direct English equivalent, but it means "continuous improvement." It can be huge differences, but is usually small tweaks that may result in only 1 to 5% improvement in measurable things like attendance or on-time payments or less tangible things like student satisfaction or reliably hitting emotional peaks in performance.

Kaizen is standardized with the Deming circle or Plan-Do-Check-Act (PDCA). It starts with a plan so that you know what you are doing. The plan is then implemented and data is collected. That data is then reviewed. Using the feedback, it is revised. Simple, right?

I was doing this long before I knew there was a name for it. This is what helped me to develop so many award-winning students in such a short period of time. It is what lead to the creation of my certification program. I knew that there were steps to success. I knew they could be quantified. I also knew that they could always be better. I saw that if I gave my students or myself feedback that was acted upon, each successive attempt would be different. If the changes were positive, they were adopted. If they were not, we reviewed and revised again until we got positive changes. If a student made a 2% improvement each week, that was an 8 to 10% improvement each month. In a year's time, the student's skill would more than double!

There is no magic to it. It's not "cheating." It's just using your old noggin to get the best results.

Keep Score

I have heard that performing assessments and keeping score is not in alignment with the sisterhood vibe of belly dance. Many people come to belly dance for the spiritual aspects, camaraderie and exercise. They say they don't want to be judged. This is a fixed mindset. Even if that IS what you and they are there for, they are also there to learn how to dance. Dance is the vehicle for self-expression, camaraderie, or exercise. It won't hurt a thing if the movement is more technically correct, artistically created, or more emotionally meaningful. It will only enhance what they came for. So keep score.

Give feedback that helps your students have more of what they came for. When they see their skill growing, they will achieve real self-esteem, not this fluffy "You're elegant and beautiful" (because I say so and let's keep your self-worth dependent upon my approval) stuff that only applies when they are wearing something shiny and are surrounded by their friends. The only way to get real self-esteem is to give students solid instruction, enthusiastic support, concrete instructions, and meaningful feedback to keep them growing so that they know when they are doing well.

The feedback isn't just for your students though. It's also for you. If you don't have a productive class, make note of that. Was it related to room temperature, feeling hungry, feeling resentful because someone hasn't paid or isn't pulling her weight? Or were you simply ill prepared? You owe it to yourself to work these things out, prepare, and do better next time. Expect that of your students and yourself and your expectations will be met.

Remember that keeping score isn't about beating yourself up or judging people. In order for it to be useful, it should be nonjudgmental. If you were late, you were late. 'Nuff said. Take note. Correct the action and move on. There is no need to turn it into something bad. It is just ineffective. So change it to something that is more productive and in alignment with your goals.

Dance, like life, is a process. Some days you do really well. You want to capitalize on that by taking note of what went well so that you can do it again. On the days that don't go so well, you can learn. But only if you keep score. So keep score.

To be clear, keeping score is not about comparing yourself to other teachers or keeping up with the Joneses. It is about comparing *your* plans to *your* outcomes. If you don't reach your goal, try something different until you do. When you reach your goal, extend the goal and move beyond it.

If you find yourself comparing yourself to other teachers, remind yourself to mind your own business! Each business is run by people with different goals, niches, motivations, personalities, resources, and experiences. It doesn't make sense to judge yourself by their yardstick or allow them to do that to you.

Take Advantage of Feedback

In about everything I do I ask for feedback. It is your greatest gift. Even if you get something back that looks nonsensical or ridiculously inappropriate, look at it mindfully before discarding it. It could contain a gem.

For example, when a new student starts class with me, I ask her to write down short-term and long-term goals. Every six months or so, I give these papers back to the whole class so that they can review them. Most of the time, they have met their short-term goal. They also realize how close they are to their long-term goals. This is a way of acknowledging their progress and encouraging them to keep going.

Feedback does the same thing for me! It's not a one-way street. My students are able to evaluate my performance too! They grade me on a Likert scale on set criteria and can also write in personal observations so they aren't confined to pre-determined subjects. This is invaluable feedback to me. It is a great way for me to see when changes are needed. It helps some students who felt like evaluations are a test to adopt a more growth-oriented mindset. It also potentially prevents premature terminations as students get a chance to voice their opinions.

Encouraging feedback from clients is also useful. It has helped me to keep long standing gigs at restaurants. When attendance falls off, I collaborate with the management to see how we can switch things up to keep it fresh. If a restaurant likes one dancer in particular or one routine, we see how we can include that more often.

Any successful business should provide two things: a quality service and a satisfying experience. Listening to feedback can help you do both of those things better.

Don't limit your definition of feedback to solicited comments. Take advantage of what flows to you naturally as well. If you overhear someone say something negative about a show, listen! If it contains concrete suggestions on what could be improved upon, by all means use it! If you get a twinge when you hear unkind gossip about you or your business, ask yourself what that twinge is trying to tell you. Is there something about your business that needs to be changed? Is there some personal growth work that you've been ignoring? Or could this be a sign that your profile is growing and people are noticing your work? Whatever it means, take note.

Take Responsibility

No matter what happens in my studio, the buck always stops at my desk. If one of my students doesn't wear underwear at a recital, I take responsibility for not making it clear that that was the standard. If a group performance is weak, I take responsibility for scheduling more rehearsals, changing the policy for who is eligible to perform, or making sure that the instruction is clear.

It's easy to get angry, point the finger, and yell at someone else. When you stand up and say, "What can I do to make this better?" it puts you in the driver's seat. Blaming makes you a victim because all you can do if someone else is in charge is sulk, ask for change, and hope that things change. When you are in charge, you can either make the needed changes or kick yourself for not doing it.

The other benefit is that it teaches your students leadership. There was nothing particularly extraordinary about my group or me when we started. We were just like anyone else. What made us fantastic was this growth-oriented, self-disciplined, self-determination approach to dance. If my actions say to my student, "I am going to give you every opportunity to learn, grow and reach your goals because I believe in you. All you have to do is your part," she will excel. Especially when she sees how fast the other gals are nipping at her heels. What I am saying is, if you take responsibility, so will they.

This works for policies as well. I read the dance boards like everyone else. I see the teachers crying for help in trying to manage their classrooms. I never had these problems early on, I created policies that I could live with and held everyone accountable to them. I took responsibility for creating them, making sure everyone knew what they were, and enforcing them. The students took responsibility for upholding them. Nobody came to me asking for an extension to pay. Nobody expected a dance slot if they didn't have good attendance and the required costume. This left me more time for teaching dance because there really just was no drama. My advice is to do the same. Take responsibility.

Now this does not mean that you take responsibility for what is not yours. There is a difference between taking responsibility and enabling. If my troupe does a poor job performing a choreography, it's appropriate for me to take responsibility for not creating something that is at their skill level, not giving them enough time to learn it, or overloading the schedule by also asking them to sew new costumes at the same time.

It would not be appropriate to take responsibility for the poor performance of one student who doesn't take time outside of class to rehearse or who is habitually late. In a case like this, the responsible thing may be to cut that student from the performance before the show. Making excuses just allows such problems to continue. This is not the standard of a successful studio.

Don't Stop Learning (Never Be the Expert in the Room)

Every organization needs a leader. Always be the leader. Never be the expert. When you are the expert, your cup is full. No more can go in. You have it all. The growth mindset tells us that we can always be more, achieve more, and learn more. Don't cut yourself off from that opportunity by assuming the role of expert.

My students taught me more about teaching than anyone. They taught me what not to do. They taught me humility, how to see through the eyes of a beginner, how to teach through my body as well as my words and actions, how to ask informative questions, and so much more. I became a much better teacher because of having an open mind and seeing people as equals.

And we are all equals. We don't have the same knowledge, talents, or thoughts, but we are equals. As such we are all teachers for each other. Some may teach us things about work, some about relationships, some about ourselves. Learning opportunities abound when you hit a block, scratch your head and say, "What do I do now?" with an air of curiosity.

Some learning is more direct. If you want to learn more about dance, go to a dance class. If you want to learn more about teaching, study the teachers you find most effective or inspiring. If you want to learn about marketing, read a book or attend a seminar. Don't be afraid to say, "I don't know." When you admit that you don't know, you open yourself to finding the answer.

Have you ever heard the Zen story Empty Your Cup? It tells the story of a famous Zen master who granted an audience to a college professor who wanted to learn about Zen. As the master quietly served tea, the professor talked on and on about Zen. As he listened, the master reached for the teapot and began pouring tea into the professor's cup until it was overflowing. The professor watched and waited for him to stop, but the tea kept flowing. Finally he said, "Stop! Stop! The cup is full and can't take anymore! The master calmly replied, "Yes, this is you. How can I show you Zen unless you first empty your cup?"

Don't be the professor. You'll limit your growth and that's not all. Do you know why it's lonely at the top? Because all the experts are up there by themselves! Remember those six emotional needs we talked about earlier? We need all of them. The more lofty we are, the less connected we are. Don't put yourself on a pedestal. It shuts off opportunities to learn as well as connect.

Don't be afraid that this will lessen your sense of importance or significance. It doesn't. It increases it. In my first job in corporate America, I had the most wonderful boss. He allowed me to be the self-starter that I am, encouraged me when I needed it, and gave me more responsibility as my skills grew. He never directly groomed me for anything and never took on a patronizing air. Yet nobody doubted his intelligence or leadership. All anyone had to do was look at the productivity ratings and advancement of his whole team to know that he got great results. He was our undeniable leader. Anyone with eyes could also see the loyalty and respect that we had for him.

Don't be afraid that you will groom students who will outshine you. As long as you continue growing they won't, and even if they do, you will feel that it is your greatest achievement. There is no downside to being a perpetual student and a fabulous leader.

Practice Professionalism and Ethics

One reason that belly dance continues to be considered one of the step-sisters of the dance world is our lack of professionalism. Sure, we have a lot of hobbyists, but that doesn't absolve us of appearing professional when we are out in public. Looking like homeless Gypsies, speaking like sailors, drinking, gossiping with students, and being overly familiar with customers and clients is a short-term strategy to fulfillment that won't likely lead to long-term business success.

Dancing may be something that you do for yourself, but it's also a business. If you want to succeed, you have to treat it like one. Leadership demands professionalism. You are the leader of your classroom and the person who has the most influence in developing your students into dancers and fellow professionals. Part of your job is to teach them professionalism and ethics. They will model themselves after you.

Professionalism includes things like speaking to everyone with respect, honoring commitments, being on time, dressing appropriately, and carrying yourself like you know what's going on.

Ethics is a code of conduct generally shared by a group of people. It is used to provide a framework of acceptable behavior. The Belly Dance Trainer code of ethics is printed here. Feel free to use it as is or modify it to suit your purposes.

The Belly Dance Trainer Code of Ethics

The Belly Dance Trainer Code of Ethics exists to create written standards designed promote honest and ethical conduct, professionalism and respect for Middle Eastern dance as an art form and to deter wrong-doing.

We recognize the importance of codifying and making known to the belly dance profession and general public the ethical principles that guide our work as Middle Eastern Dance professionals and Belly Dance Trainers.

The principles of this Code are expressed in broad statements to guide ethical decision-making. These statements provide a framework; they cannot and do not dictate conduct to cover particular situations.

Our Values

Colleagues: Certified belly dance instructors shall treat dance colleagues with professionalism and refrain from public defamation.

Practice Limits: Certified belly dance instructors shall teach Middle Eastern dance within the limits of their training and competence.

Promotion: Instructors always shall be honest about the nature of their belly dance education when referring to it to the general public, in the media, or to their clients.

Legal Responsibility: Instructors shall credit sources for choreography, music, photography, and intellectual property when possible. Certified belly dance instructors will only take credit for property that they create. Further, instructors shall not use, teach, or distribute property that does not belong to them without written permission from the owner.

Client Welfare: Instructors shall guard the individual rights and personal dignity of each student. Certified belly dance instructors shall not engage in discriminatory practices in regard to age, weight, religion, disability, race, sexual orientation or any other protected status.

Client Privacy: Instructors agree to respect the privacy of fellow belly dance students and professionals and responsibly use personal information gained from that relationship.

Professionalism: Instructors shall make every attempt to be aware of acceptable workplace standards, including pay, and shall not lower the standards nor engage in workplace practices that degrade the respect for the art form, working conditions, or pay.

Quality Control: Instructors are obligated to report violations of the Code of Ethics by fellow members to Taaj the Belly Dance Trainer (SM). Taaj shall review any reported incidents and shall determine whether the offense rises to the level of a violation.

Infractions

Consequences for infractions will depend on the severity of the infraction. Consequences can include a warning, suspension, or removal of certification. Decisions are made solely by Taaj the Belly Dance Trainer (SM) and do not require proof. If a preponderance of the evidence strongly suggests that an infraction has occurred, that's all the evidence that is required. Decisions are final. There is no appeal. Reinstatement decisions will be made on a case-by-case basis.

There are some articles that may be noticeably absent from the BDT Code of Ethics. For instance, it's common in many dance circles to stay loyal to your dance teacher and not go to other studios. It's common to respect the turf of other dancers and not solicit for business where there is already a dancer employed. I actually don't agree with either of these, for several reasons.

I believe competition makes us all stronger by forcing us to be professional, mindful of price, and keep the quality up. I also believe that in order to grow, students should take classes from as many teachers as possible. Finally, I believe that the business owner has a right to decide what is best for his establishment. Rotating dancers is generally good for business and keeps the customers coming in. This means that we all have a potential place of employment.

When you have a growth mindset, you don't see your colleagues as competitors, but potential allies. Requiring a noncompete contract of your students, whether formally or informally doesn't occur to you because you accept that not every client is a good fit for you. Not every job is the right job for you, and no matter what, there is enough for everybody. Nobody is truly competition because nobody is you. You have your own unique way of dancing. You have your own look and style. As long as you keep improving your dance skills, professionalism, presentation, sales pitch, business acumen, and other related skills, you will have a place in the game.

Network

Belly dance is a social business. If you look around, you will see that the teachers who tend to have the biggest presence are also the ones who do the best job of networking. It's a good old girls' world. If you want to break in, you have to see and be seen by people who will support you. If you are extroverted, this is probably a fun part of business that you do without thinking about it. If you are introverted, your networking skills probably could use a boost.

Like everything, networking is a skill that can be practiced and learned. Just let your love for what you do shine through. Be genuine and people will connect with that. It doesn't have to be fake and shouldn't be.

When done well, networking flows easily. It's just about finding a way to connect with people who love what you love. You can do this by sharing your ideas in articles for your website or submitting to print publications, e-zines, or other people's blogs. You can comment on other people's blogs (preferably high traffic sites), social networking pages (like Facebook and Twitter), and of course, on your own social networking sites.

Post announcements about your events. People need to know where to see you dance and teach. You will want to post favorable comments about events that you have attended. Share the love and it comes back to you.

Post photos and videos of yourself! The way to become a recognizable name and face is to be seen. Most should be photos of you dancing because you want people to associate you with dance. It's fine to post other pictures of you hanging out with your dance friends at dance events, wearing dance gear, or shopping for dance costumes. Just make sure that the message you are always sending with whatever you post is, "I am the dancer/teacher you are looking for."

Post photos and videos of people you admire as well. A little appreciation goes a long way. People like people who like them. They like people who like the same people they like. If you show some love to "Shadia" by letting the world know she had a great performance or is teaching an upcoming workshop, that energy is more likely to come back around to you.

Before you put anything out for other people to see, ask yourself, "Is this representative of how I want people to see me as a business person?" If it is, go ahead and release it. If it isn't, don't. For those who are not sure, let me give you some general advice. Don't post pictures of your cute adorable pets or children. They show a side of you that is commonplace. You want other people to see you as The Incomparable Show Girl. When you are smiling in your garden with your cat, you are the girl next door. When you are fresh from the child birthing bed, you may feel like Wonder Woman, but you are just another human. Always, always, always have your show face on in public.

You know that old saying about religion and politics? That still stands true in business. Don't post things that reflect your views on religion and politics. It may seem that belly dance is a big Girls Club and that we're all friends. It does tend to be social and that can cause you to let your guard down. Don't! If your fans disagree with your positions on abortion, gay marriage, guns, or whatever, they may desert you. You are certainly entitled to your opinions, but this is not the place to post them. While you are dancing, you are always conducting business. That business is to be beautiful, entertaining, instructive, and fun.

If you are serious about building a lasting and successful business, I'd also say don't post things that show your human frailty. We all have moments when we are a little bit crazy, lonely, angry, or maybe even drunk. If you need to reach out at those times, do it on your personal site. Do it with your real friends, not your business contacts. Genuineness is a rare feature that we rarely see in others. It is a necessary component to intimacy, and you can't truly create intimacy with strangers. What will most likely happen is that you give people a reason to judge you and turn away from you. It's not worth the risk to your business or your mental health.

See every contact as a potential networking opportunity, whether you are buying groceries, dropping your kids off at school, singing in the church choir, or standing the wings waiting to go on stage. Be ready with a smile, a business card, and your ten-second elevator speech.

What's a ten-second elevator speech? This is your previously rehearsed, but naturally sounding answer to the question, "So what do you do?" when you meet some stranger in an elevator or anywhere else. You don't want to say, "Oh, I am a belly dancer." You want to give them enough information that they will say either, "Tell me more!" or better yet "You're hired!"

The secret to doing this successfully is to first write it out and rehearse it until it flows naturally. You DON'T want it to sounds salesy. You DON'T want to pitch a product or service. You DON'T want to talk about yourself. You just give them your best stuff and invite them to bite. If they don't, you either need to go back and hone your pitch or understand that they just aren't prospects. After all, belly dance isn't toilet paper. It's not something everyone needs.

To create your ten-second elevator speech, start by brainstorming what you offer (services and/or products). Then list the benefits of these services. Next list why you are the best person to provide this service. Finally list some hard core information about what makes you so great. In other words, avoid hyperbole.

Don't worry about writing in complete sentences or getting it just right. Hopefully you will be revising this over time letting it get better and better.

Some examples are:

Hi. My name is Taaj. I am the owner of an award-wining dance studio (this is my "why I am great" piece) where we teach women how to have fun and gain self-esteem (this is the benefit) through belly dance (this is what I do).

Hello. I'm Taaj, and I help women who want to become award-winning belly dancers (this is my target audience) reach their contest goals (this is what I do and also the benefit). When fifteen of my students won forty-seven trophies in five years, I knew I had a winning formula! (This is what makes me great) and now I coach dancers from all over.

I'm Taaj. I write books (what I do and also why you should listen to me) that help dance teachers streamline their classrooms (benefit), increase their productivity (benefit), and increase their income (benefit) while also having more fun (benefit).

Hi, have you ever seen the movie My Big Fat Greek Wedding where everyone is dancing and partying in this lively foreign style? (This paints a picture and builds a connection –assuming that the person can relate to the example). That is what I do. (This is what I do and why you should choose me). I am the belly dancer that starts the party (benefit) at weddings, graduations, birthdays and retirements and makes sure everyone has a good time (benefit).

As you can see, there are different styles. You can have a more formal pitch or one that is more conversational. Play with it and keep it as natural sounding as possible.

You may want to develop two elevator speeches- one ten-second pitch for everyone you meet and one thirty-second pitch for those you already know have some interest in belly dance. For warm prospects, it could be appropriate to talk a bit more about what makes you passionate about what you do and end with a call to action like, "May I send you more information?" or "Do you know anyone who could benefit from my services?"

Leave a Trail of Success

Success is hard to hide. It leaves trails. Jamila Salimpour and Ibrahim Farrah didn't have to advertise their greatness because they both had hundreds of walking, talking advertisements – their students! When the bulk of the teachers showing up on the workshop circuit belong to one of two teachers, people take note.

Your work will speak for you too. Make it the best that it can be. Create something that is a shining testament to your vision, your talent, your beliefs- you! It could be a fabulous hafla, a kick butt annual workshop, award winning students, a lucrative studio, or a vision of beauty. We are always in the process of creating our brand. Do it intentionally and it will work to enhance your business.

Obtain and Use Testimonials

Testimonials are glowing statements from satisfied customers that tell you and others what fabulous work you have done. Testimonials work well because they are third party endorsements. We may not believe what YOU tell us you can do because you are in business to perpetuate your business. You might tell us anything. On the other hand, someone who has nothing to gain is a much more believable source. I am more likely to trust that what you did for her is available to me as well.

If someone gives you an unsolicited verbal testimonial, either ask if they would put it in writing or ask if you can quote them. Don't use a testimonial without permission. Sometimes people want to maintain their privacy.

Not all testimonials are worth sharing. A great testimonial is specific so that others can see what you can do for them. For example, "You were great" is nice to hear, but it doesn't tell anyone what provoked that comment so it's not useful. Are they talking about customer service, timeliness, emotional sensitivity, price, the overall look, dance ability, what? A weak testimonial is almost as bad as none at all.

If you get a mixed testimonial, only use the part that you'd like others to see. Something like *Ramble, ramble, good stuff, ramble ...*

should be cut of the rambling bits so that the useful parts are highlighted. There is no obligation to use everything.

Never Believe Your Own Hype

Promotion is a necessary part of any business. You have to show people that you are spectacular in order to keep the business running. But don't ever believe your own hype. Once you start thinking you are special, you lose connection with others and also to your work.

In that head space, work can become about maintaining that image instead of creating, having fun, connecting, growing, and expressing yourself. It can get really easy to step on others to elevate yourself, separate yourself from those who also have something to offer, harshly judge yourself, and fall back into a fixed mindset.

THINK LIKE A SUCCESSFUL PERSON

I don't know who created the meme that so succinctly pinpointed the differences in thinking between those who are successful and those who aren't, but they did a great job. Here is the list:

Successful People	Unsuccessful People
Have a sense of gratitude	Have a sense of entitlement
Compliment others	Criticize others
Give other people credit for their victories	Take all the credit for their victories
Forgive others	Hold a grudge
Accept responsibility for their failures	Blame others for their failures
Read every day	Watch TV every day
Talk about ideas	Talk about other people
Share information and data	Hoard information and data
Exude joy	Are driven by fear

Embrace change	Fear change
Keep a "to-do" or project list	Have a pile of unfinished business
Keep a journal	Say they keep a journal but don't
Want others to succeed	Secretly want others to fail
Keep a "to-be" list	Don't know what they want to be
Sets goals and develop life plans	Fly by the seat of their pants
Continuously learn	Avoid asking questions to hide what they don't know
Operation from a transformational perspective	Operate from a transactional perspective

Before you shoot me down for including something that you do, I would ask you to look at the big picture. People are seldom 100% of this or that. We all cross the line in some ways. Remember the goal is constant improvement. We are all works in progress and the work never ends. The point of this section is to gauge where you are and get you moving toward a path of growth so that you can achieve your dreams. If you think you need some adjustment, make the change. If you don't agree, keep your old ways and re-evaluate mindfully later. If your habits are working for you, keep them.

Another thing that I would add to this list is that successful people are mindful of how appearances impact perception. It may be small-minded and petty to judge a book by its cover, but that should not stop you from presenting an attractive cover so that you can garner that business. After all, you can't walk through a door that's not open.

It's one thing to know within yourself that you are more than your work, your look, or any single feature. It's quite another to ask someone to step outside of their comfort zone and into your reality so that they can give you their business.

Your language, promotional materials, photographs, dance style, body, make-up, costuming, demeanor, socialization – everything -- makes a statement about you. You won't go wrong if you stick to choices that are rated G, appropriate for the boardroom, and are nicely packaged.

For instance, I was walking out of work one day toward the parking lot. I was wearing a dress, heels, and light make-up -- the usual for work wear. A lady called out from behind me as I was getting into my truck and said laughingly, "I knew you were going to get into that truck!" I looked quizzically at her without speaking because I wasn't sure to what she was referring. My off-color bumper sticker? My politically charged license plate?

She replied, "Well, you're just dressed so nice." Ah, I got it. She was making a judgment about me because she thought I looked nice and my farm truck didn't. This is how people think. In the big picture of life, it doesn't matter a hoot that I often drive my farm truck instead of my sports car to work because I live an hour away. It's cheaper to put regular gas in the truck than premium in my sports car, and I'd rather not put the miles on the sports car. When she sees that I don't match her perception of what it looks like to be successful, she makes a judgment.

This lady wasn't a client, or even a potential client, but she could have been. So the moral of the story is, don't let this happen to you. I made three mistakes that day: the bumper sticker, the license plate, and the mismatch in appearance. As much as possible, when you are in a position to be seen by potential clients, always look successful. Look 100% congruent with how you want clients to see you. No hair rollers, foul language, drinking on the job, gossiping, public displays of affection, or anything that might create an impression other than, "Wow! SHE is the belly dancing goddess!"

Obviously when we are talking about something as expensive as a vehicle, you may not have the option to have two cars or to upgrade the one you have. Just do the best that you can to project the image of success in every way possible. If you are like me and don't care a whit about appearances, you may find this is not easy nor is it second nature. It may be helpful to view your stage and business persona as a separate entity. Feel free to shed your professional persona when you are in the privacy of your own home and with family and friends.

Say "Yes" to Money

I don't know who started the rumor that a starving artist was sexy or that starving was a necessary part of creativity. I'd bet that whomever it was never made any money. If you want to pay your bills, you have to say yes to money and no to "opportunities" that don't pay.

Every time you say, "Sure, I will do X for little or nothing" you get more of that. Those people tell other people, "I hired a belly dancer for my sister's wedding for $15" and then everyone else wants that. When that happens, you can't really stand there wondering why nobody wants to pay you a decent wage. You have created the situation for yourself.

You. Deserve. To. Be. Paid. Well. Got it? All professionals do. Belly dance lessons and entertainment are LUXURIES. You paid a lot of money to learn what you know. You invested a lot of years. You learned a lot of things to make it this far. You deserve to be compensated for that, so ask for a fair wage. If you don't value your own talent, why should your clients?

People understand that anything that isn't food, shelter, water, clothing, or transportation is extra. In order to have it, sacrifices may have to be made in other areas of their lives. They do it for their animals. They do it for their kids. Remember that that beginner's ballet class is $33 per hour! Why should you make less than a ballet teacher?

Saying yes to money isn't just about setting an appropriate fee. It's about allowing yourself to be successful. Money is how we keep score. It doesn't make sense really, but since it's what we do, having a wad of disposable income at the end of each week helps us to feel good about what we do, keep doing it, and feel that we are good at it. Who doesn't want that?

While I am on the topic of money, let me say a bit about the law of attraction. Maybe you believe in it or maybe you don't, but one thing is true. Your subconscious will not allow you to have or to be that which you despise. What I mean is, if you believe things like "Money is the root of all evil" or "Rich people are greedy," or even "You can't make money belly dancing." you are never going to make much money dancing. Your subconscious won't let you because you've deemed those things undesirable.

Money is not evil. It doesn't make people wicked. It's just a tool that people use to make them more of what they already are. If you are generous, you can be more generous. If you are selfish, you will have more opportunities to be selfish. If you are wasteful, arrogant, driven, passionate, careful, anxious, or happy, money will allow you to be more of that. If you find yourself giving people with money a hard time, check yourself. You can't have what you despise. I want you to be successful, if for no other reason than that it will allow you to do more of what you love. So say yes to money. Be grateful when it shows up -- for yourself and others -- and you will get more of it.

Never See an End Game

"Never see an end game" is another way of saying don't put a cap on what can be achieved. Some people say things like, "After X, I will retire" or "I can't make more than $X." There is no cap to what you can do unless you create it. As long as the carrot is still dangling out there in front of you and you keep reaching for it, you can and will achieve greater and greater heights.

Success isn't about achieving goals. If it were, there would be a lot more happy people out there sitting on their laurels. Success is about having a life of meaning and meeting your whys. It's about making connections, feeling important, having enough money to feel secure, doing different things, growing, and sharing. If you do that through your work, you'll have very fulfilling work. So have fun now while you are reaching for your goals. When you have achieved those, set new ones.

Don't be afraid to go for the impossible. After all, what is impossible is only impossible until someone does it. Remember the story of Roger Bannister and the four-minute mile? Nobody believed that it was humanly possible to run a mile in four minutes or less. Doctors even said that it would be lethal if it were attempted. Yet Roger Bannister did it in 1954. What's more, many others did it quickly after he did.

Go big. Why not? Remember, like money, success just makes you more of what you already are. Start a trend for a new kind of dance pants, or create a new belly dance fusion style, or be the first national belly dance studio franchise. Energy and enthusiasm create expansion. You're here because you love dance, right? So, let your love flow. Success is always the natural byproduct.

Align Your Conflicting Values

Everyone has conflicting values from time to time. This creates a problem because nobody wants to be at odds with herself, particularly because this is just the type of thing that puts the brakes on our plans. If you feel you are in a situation where, no matter what you do, you will create bad feelings, self-doubt, low self-esteem, or negative repercussions of any sort, it's easy to go into "stuck mode" and do nothing.

There are a lot of ways that conflicting values can show up in your life. To use a dance example, let's say that you're thinking about teaching your first workshop in another state, but have mixed feelings about it. Your conflicted feelings are a big clue that something about this situation is in conflict with your values. Pay attention to that.

Let's say you look at this situation and realize that you want to do the workshop because you feel like it is the next logical step in your dance career and will bring you good exposure. You know you're not getting any younger and if you don't start now, this may not ever happen for you. You are so grateful that someone would even ask you to teach anywhere. Finally, the offer is a fair one.

On the other hand, you don't want to do it because your kids are at an age when you don't want to leave them for the weekend. You also don't like the rushed feeling of traveling, meeting so many people, feeling pressured to deliver a fabulous workshop and performance, rushing back home, going to work the next day, and keeping up with everything you missed while you were away from home. So, how can you be true to yourself if you are in conflict?

When you are confronted with situations like this, look a little deeper for the root issue and see if there is a win/win way of seeing things. For instance, in the above example it looks like you both want and don't want to do out-of-state workshops. Is that really the case? How else can you look at those facts? Let's make a list of the "facts" and see.

- I want to advance my dance career.
- Teaching workshops are a way to advance my career.
- I may not have the chance to teach workshops if I don't start now.
- This teaching offer is a fair one.
- I don't want to leave my kids alone for the weekend.
- Traveling tires me out, increases my anxiety, and makes me feel pressured.
- Teaching and dancing for others inspires and renews me.

If you look at the issues above objectively, you may see that there are some statements that aren't facts. This can give you some room to reinterpret your conclusions and perhaps come up with something that you feel will give you a green light to go forward. One example is the statement, "I may not have the chance to teach workshops if I don't start now." How many older teachers do you see on the workshop circuit? If you are looking through the same eyes that I am, you're going to see many fine examples of this. One of the beauties of the belly dance community is its claim to support women of all ages, sizes, and colors. So, as long as you have the fitness level to do the job, this shouldn't be a huge factor in when you could start.

Another statement that could be seen as a gray area is "I don't want to leave my kids alone for the weekend." I am sure you wouldn't leave your kids totally alone and unsupervised. If that's the case, is there anyone who could be a suitable, short-term substitute for you? A family member, perhaps? Is there something you would miss by being away for a weekend? If so, is there some way to do that during the week? Is there any way your child and a caretaker could come with you? What would you want your child to have that you feel could not be provided by someone else in your absence?

Many of our objections are not black and white. There is usually another way of seeing things if we step outside the box. Sometimes our excuses are not valid at all. Sometimes they are ways of talking ourselves out of following our dreams, being successful, or stepping into the limelight. Be sure to check out those possibilities as well.

By examining the issues, you could come to any one of the following conclusions that would allow you to move forward:

- My family is the most important thing to me. I will never be able to get back my children's young years, yet I have lots of time to pursue dance. I will wait to do workshops.
- This is not a big deal. It's one workshop and one weekend, not the rest of my life. Of course I want to go! Of course the kids will be okay with their father! I need to allow myself to enjoy my life, expand my opportunities, and stop making excuses for why I don't deserve this. Everyone and everything is going to be fine.
- I am important. My family is important. I don't see why we can't make a family event out of it and they can all come with me. It's not that far away, and it will be the best of both worlds.

It might help to go back to your why. Why do you want to teach workshops? Is there another way to meet this need? How does staying home with your children meet your emotional needs or your why? Is this an effective way to get that need met?

It could be that by looking at your why you discover that teaching bigger audiences of new students gives you a sense of significance that you don't get from teaching at home. Or maybe it's an increased sense of contribution or connection. If those are among your top two needs, going may be more important than it appears.

Maybe being with your family is how you fill your need for connection. Or perhaps you are afraid that if you aren't there, they will connect with someone else (creating a loss of safety). Or maybe it's about needing to create an image of yourself as the perfect mother so that you can feel significant.

If an honest look at your situation reveals that some things are out of balance, address the issues so that your values can be in alignment again. For example, if your need for connection, safety, or significance dominate your life, this may indicate that you rely heavily on others to feel happy and complete. Perhaps it is time to investigate ways to get validation from within. If your need for adventure, growth, or contribution dominate your life, this may show that it's time to build intimacy and relationships with others.

If you look at all the self-help books and memoirs out there, you will see that most focus on personal obstacles. They tell stories of how someone became better than they were by using the lessons that came from their life experiences. If you are investing time in developing your dance career, why not let that be a teaching experience for you too? There is so much you can learn about yourself. You can grow both personally and professionally by just paying attention. When you find yourself in a stuck place, realign your goals and values and watch the energy move you forward again.

Become Comfortable With Discomfort

If you are a person who likes routine and predictability, I am going to ask you to get out of your comfort zone. Why? Because comfort equals stagnation. Entertainment is a dynamic business. If you stand still, your business will pass you by. You may have a handful of loyal students and clients who stand by you, but America craves what's fresh, new, and bold.

Learn to recognize your own restlessness. Use that energy to keep moving, creating, and growing. I am not suggesting that it's necessary to chase after the latest fads, although some will find that attractive. You can go deep instead of wide. Find juicy new layers to doing what you already do. Find ways of reaching different or bigger audiences. Play with costuming, lighting, makeup, or music to discover new ways to display your ideas. Broaden your network to share and expose yourself to new ideas.

Or perhaps it's time to rest. This doesn't mean quit or take time off necessarily. It could mean that you just take it easy for a while. We all know dancers who go, go, go and then burn out. They leave dance altogether because they gave it their all until there was nothing left to give. The world loses a great resource and the dancer loses her love. Nobody wins from that situation.

Discomfort is your friend. It tells you that you have been standing still too long. It's saying things need to change. It's saying that the natural lifecycle for what was is at an end. It's time to rest or renew. Don't fight it. Listen to it. Accept it. Know that when it shows up, it's just saying, "Hey! It's time for something different." Thomas Edison put it this way, "Discontent is the first necessity of progress. Show me a thoroughly satisfied man and I'll show you a failure."

Remove Mental Barriers to Success

If you divided success into individual components, you might find that the smallest piece is luck followed by talent. A huge chunk of it would be follow-through and diligence. The most important piece would be a can-do mental attitude. Henry Ford was right when he said, "Whether you think you can or think you can't – you're right."

I've taught enough students in my time to know that the major difference between a dancer who reaches her goals and one who doesn't, is the belief that it is possible. I routinely gave students technical challenges that were supposed to be beyond their abilities, delivering them with the expectation that the work was easy. Since they didn't know it was supposed to be hard, they kept at it until they mastered the challenge.

Children don't know what is impossible. They climb, jump, explore, and go, go, go until they learn from adults that things are dangerous or impossible. Slowly we all begin to pull back, doubt ourselves, and be more careful. Sometimes to the point of not daring at all.

Dare.

Whatever is holding you back, acknowledge it. Embrace it. Thank it for wanting to protect you from heartache, failure, or whatever its purpose is. Then let it go. However well meaning your fears are, they can't protect you from life. Life is full of pain, disappointments, and regret. You'll get your fill whether you dare or not, so dare. You have nothing to lose by stepping into your power and going for it. You have so much to gain.

Here's how to know that you have mental barriers to success:

- Not having concrete plans
- Not following through with your plans
- Talking yourself out of doing things that you think will get you to success
- Thinking other people are sabotaging you somehow
- Believing you have bad luck or a curse
- Making fun of people who have what you want
- Attributing other people's success to luck
- Telling yourself you're too busy to pursue your dreams
- Spending time researching or learning about success rather than achieving it
- Giving yourself excuses why you can't succeed (like you're too short, fat, ugly, old, inexperienced, shy, old-fashioned, poor, etc.)
- Feeling guilty when something good happens to you
- Being indecisive or being unable to say no
- Becoming hard to be around when something good happens to you
- Striving so hard for perfection that you can't get started at all
- Focusing on your weaknesses or challenges and downplaying positive attributes
- Idolizing others and feeling you can never reach their achievements
- Doing things to hide from others (like acting timid, bullying others to cover up your insecurities, acting subservient,

dressing down, making yourself the butt of jokes)
- Pretending to be something you are not
- Being outrageous, anti-social, rebellious, or exhibitionistic so that you aren't taken seriously
- Being stingy with money, praise, or resources
- Judging people by their resources instead of their character
- Being unable to take constructive criticism
- Seeing set-backs and failures as the end of the world rather than keeping them in perspective
- Lying and exaggerating
- Being unable to treat yourself well
- Clinging to routine and the need to keep things the same
- Finding it hard to laugh or find joy in your work

We all have barriers to success. For some of us, they are present all the time. For others, they pop up in certain situations. For example, I may be confident in all areas of my life except when my dad comes into the picture. Then suddenly I become a helpless little girl. Or maybe I am successful in all areas of my life except financially.

Barriers are created in the mind. They are not real. They can be eradicated as easily as they are formed. When you encounter evidence that you have hit a barrier, you owe it to yourself to tear it down. Most of these come from childhood programming -- often from well-meaning parents. Yet you are not a child anymore. These programs no longer serve you. So it's time to write a new script and put you back into the driver's seat of your own life.

Some people may hesitate to remove their barriers to success because it means they will have to take responsibility for what happens with their lives. That's a really scary place to be if you have never been there before. It's also incredibly thrilling. Imagine YOU are in the driver's seat! You can go anywhere and do anything just by deciding to do it. So, why not remove your barriers, press the gas pedal and go?

It's beyond the scope of this book to get into how to remove mental barriers; however, if you'd like some one-on-one help with this, please feel free to contact me at taaj@rocketmail.com. I love doing change work with people and would love to work with you.

If you'd like to check out some self-help resources to remove mental barriers to success, try one or more of these:

Achor, Shawn. *The Happiness Advantage: The Seven Principles of Positive Psychology That Fuel Success and Performance At Work.* Crown Business, 2010.

Carnegie, Dale. *How to Win Friends and Influence People.* Pocket Books, 1998.

Covey, Stephen R. *The 7 Habits of Highly Effective People: Powerful Lessons in Personals Change.* Simon and Schuster., 2013.

Dweck, Carol. *Mindset: The New Psychology of Success.* Ballantine Books, 2007.

Eker. T. Harv. *Secrets of the Millionaire Mind: Mastering the Inner Game of Wealth.* Harper Business, 2005.

Hay, Louise. *You Can Heal Your Life.* Hay House, 1984.

Hill, Napoleon. *Think and Grow Rich: The Original 1937 Unedited Edition.* Napoleon Hill Foundation, 2012.

Ortner, Nick. *The Tapping Solution: A Revolutionary System for Stress-Free Living.* Hay House, 2013.

Ravikant, Kamal. *Love Yourself Like Your Life Depends On It.* Createspace, 2012.

Robbins, Anthony. *Awaken the Giant Within: How to Take Immediate Control of Your Mental, Emotional, Physical and Financial Destiny.* Free Press, 1992.

As you move toward a successful career, never forget that success is an inner game. What is inside is reflected outside. If you don't like the outside, you'll get far more bang for your buck by changing the inside. If you try to work from the outside in, you may find yourself with a lot of visible signs of success, but a lack of satisfaction and fulfillment. These resources can help you strengthen your mind so that your body can do the heavy lifting.

Enjoy the Ride

The best advice I can give to anyone embarking on a new enterprise or breathing new life into an old one is to enjoy the ride. Every experience has something to teach us if we have the eyes to see it and the ears to hear it. Each experience only has the meaning we give it so make it a positive, empowering one.

Remember that teaching, like success, is a quest. It is not something that you ever arrive at. It's a process that continues to unfold. No matter what happens, decide to enjoy the ride and your belly dance experience will be a thrilling one. If you embrace an attitude of constant improvement, you will become more efficient, productive, and profitable as well.

If you are still on doubt as to whether teaching is for you, consider Mark Twain. He said, "Twenty years from now you will be more disappointed by the things that you didn't do than by the ones you did do. So throw off the bowlines. Sail away from the safe harbor. Catch the trade winds in your sails. Explore. Dream. Discover."

ABOUT THE AUTHOR

Taaj is an award-winning dancer, teacher, and troupe director who has performed in Egypt and taught across the United States. Taaj is co-creator of the international dance publication, *Zaghareet!* Her articles have been published in every major print and online belly dance magazine. This is her fourth belly dance book.

Taaj began teaching seriously in 2001. From 2002- 2007, her students won forty-seven trophies from competitions in four states. Taaj took what she learned from coaching those students and turned it into The Belly Dance Trainer Method so that others could benefit from her champion-producing strategies. Her passion is helping others become the best that they can be. Visit her at www.thebellydancetrainer.com

TAAJ

www.ingramcontent.com/pod-product-compliance
Lightning Source LLC
Chambersburg PA
CBHW070528030426
42337CB00016B/2151